Pets and Puppies

Monica Easton

Pets

and

Puppies

Monica Easton

Matador
9 Priory Business Park,
Wistow Road, Kibworth Beauchamp,
Leicestershire, LE8 0RX
Tel: 0116 279 2299
Email: books@troubador.co.uk
Web: www.troubador.co.uk/matador
Twitter: @matadorbooks

ISBN 978 1789015 690

British Library Cataloguing in Publication Data.
A catalogue record for this book is available from the British Library.

Printed and bound in the UK by TJ International, Padstow, Cornwall
Typeset in 12pt Aldine401 BT by Troubador Publishing Ltd, Leicester, UK

Matador is an imprint of Troubador Publishing Ltd

To my family, Chris, Julie, Mark and David, for their support over the years with a house full of animals, and to the late Muriel Fry for introducing me to puppy-walking.

Contents

Introduction

For my fourth birthday I was given a white rabbit which I called Snowball. He might have looked fluffy and cuddly but, in reality, he was far from it; not a suitable pet for a child my age. My uncle Vic, who had a farm, swopped him for some bantams and two goslings. The bantams were reasonably friendly, but independent. The goslings were much tamer than the bantams. We had them from a day old, so they were happy to be with people and could be hand fed. (I named them Doody and Dozy – these seemed fabulous names at the age of four, but I'm not so sure about them now.) They came when I called them and followed me down the garden path to the gate at the end. This led to an area of rough grass where they could help themselves to a variety of green stuff and then happily follow me back home to their house and run when I called them.

This menagerie continued to grow. We added Tommy the tortoise when I was about eight and my eleventh birthday present was a green and yellow budgie called Silky, sourced once again by my uncle Vic. It looked beautiful but, however hard we tried to train it, we had no success in teaching it to speak.

Trix, my parents' dog, was my companion and friend throughout my childhood so it was a very sad day when she died. I was fourteen at the time. We all missed having a dog around and so within a few weeks Skip, an eight-week-old Cairn terrier, had arrived. A lively dog, she loved to play ball. Very much a teenager's dog.

My love of animals must be hereditary. Looking at old photographs I think nearly every other one has a picture of one of my aunts, uncles or cousins with some animal such as a cat, dog or chicken. In fact, my favourite photograph was taken with my cousins on Uncle Vic's farm. We were paddling in a shallow part of the River Loddon that ran through the farm. With us are half a dozen cows that had come along for a drink of water. I don't think health and safety would approve of the situation now, but we survived with no ill effects and had a lovely memorable afternoon.

I went to Earley St Peter's Primary School and at age eleven transferred to St Joseph's Convent Secondary School in Reading. I left school at seventeen and went to work at Jealott's Hill, an agricultural research station near Bracknell. This was where I met Chris. I worked in the botany section and he worked in the chemistry department, but we met playing tennis (the only sport that I was any good at) on the on-site tennis courts. We got married in 1966 and bought a three-bed semi-detached house in Charvil, a village about three miles from Woodley. We were both at work and so didn't have any pets, not even a goldfish in a bowl. It wasn't until 1972, when our first child Julie was a year old and I was a full-time mum and housewife, that we could consider adding a pet to our family. This turned out to be the first of many and this book tells their stories.

Rusk, where
the story begins

F un-loving, football-playing, scruffy looking
Rusk is where the story begins, as she was our
first much-loved pet. We got her when our
eldest child, Julie, was just one year old.

We had always planned to have a pet dog at some
point and it seemed a good time to get a puppy so the
two could grow up together. As this was before the
age of the internet, my husband Chris and I began
our search with a visit to the local library, a Victorian
brick-built building with twisted chimneys and a
cluster of small rooms filled with children's books
that were joined to a much bigger terrapin area

containing the adult section. This was a rare visit for me as I am not a great reader and I felt much more at home with a room full of animals than one full of books. Visits to the library as the children got older were definitely going to be Chris's domain. In the end, we borrowed several 'doggy' books and spent many happy evenings after Julie had gone to bed poring over them to decide which breed to get. The pages soon became full of carefully torn pieces of paper marking our possible choices and were revisited many times whilst we considered the pros and cons of each favoured breed. We did have some clear ideas about the type of dog that we wanted. Our specifications were that it had to be:

a. a small dog, which wouldn't take up too much room, and a bonus – my parents would be able to look after it if we needed them to.
b. good with children – we had Julie, who was a year old, and were planning to have more.
c. one that didn't moult – I'm not too enthusiastic about housework, so the fewer dog hairs floating around the house the better.
d. a bitch – for no other reason than, as a family, we had always had bitches.

In the end we were left with two paper bookmarks still in place. On our shortlist were two terriers. Terriers are small, wiry dogs that are generally very active. They were originally bred to control small animals both over and underground in burrows and holes and are considered to be fearless. Our favourites were the Border terrier, a darker brown-coloured dog with black highlights, and the lighter caramel-coloured Lakeland terrier. The eventual winner was the Lakeland terrier.

We wanted to get our puppy through a reputable source and so our next move was to contact the Kennel Club which kept updated lists of recognised breeders for any type of dog you might want. I telephoned them to put in my request and the lady at the end of the phone promised to put a list of breeders of Lakeland terriers in the post for us. It took about a week for the list to arrive, by which time we were eager to continue with our search. The list covered the whole country and, much as I really wanted a Lakeland terrier, I was not keen to travel miles in our old Morris Minor in order to find one. We felt very lucky that there was a breeder only about eight miles away in Wokingham, and we arranged to go and see her dogs.

We knocked at the door and all the dogs, which were in the kitchen, started barking. The breeder arrived to open the door and, with one short command of "Be quiet!", there was instant silence. I was very impressed with her control of her lively pack. She had several dogs and bred from both Lakeland terriers and shih-tzu, which have so much hair that it is difficult to tell the front from the back. They were lovely, but we still preferred the Lakeland terriers. When we went in she brought some of the dogs into the lounge to meet us. They were playful and friendly the whole time we were there and were great fun. We found the breeder to be friendly and kind and loved the way she handled these energetic and fun dogs. We definitely felt that we could trust her and provisionally booked a pup from the next litter.

It was not long before the next litter was born. We went to see the pups when they were a few weeks old. The mum and four pups came into the lounge to greet us. They were four little bundles of fun that rough-and-tumbled all around our feet. We were smitten already. There were two dogs and two bitches in the litter. Both bitches were a light tan colour but one had a black saddle marking. The breeder wanted to keep that one as it had the better markings and she wanted to show it, so we quite happily had the other bitch as we just wanted a pet. We had to wait until she was nine weeks old and had had her first injections before we could collect her and take her home. At the time, I decided that I would never be able to breed and sell dogs. To hand over a puppy to a complete stranger when they were only a few weeks old after spending hours rearing them, hopeful that their future home would be good, was not something I would want to do. We knew that once she had had her first season, we would have her spayed.

Lakeland terriers have wiry, curly hair. At nine weeks, our puppy's hair was already quite curly, and she had shaggy eyebrows hanging over her eyes and plenty of hair on the end of her muzzle, along with a lithe, wiry body and a tail that wagged almost continually. We were delighted to be bringing her home and had an expectant audience waiting for us when we arrived. My parents had been looking after Julie for us the evening we collected our puppy and were eagerly awaiting our return. Everyone loved the new arrival and wanted a pat or a cuddle. When Julie saw her for the first time the next morning, she was very excited, looked at her and said, "A bear!"

The new puppy was restricted to the kitchen and garden until she was house-trained, and everyone was keen to help me settle her into her new home, whilst I was just a little nervous that our recently dog-proofed garden wasn't quite dog-proofed enough and our excited, playful puppy might escape. We had put new six-foot fence panels all the way round and I was sure she couldn't jump that high. I needn't have worried. Rusk was perfectly happy in the Easton household and the complete new fencing made the garden totally dog-proof.

Naming our dog was a task we had to do. We didn't want to use a name that would normally be given to people and began thinking about ideas that suited her character and how she looked. In the end the name came quite quickly. At the time Julie was eating a baby's rusk as she had just enough teeth to crunch through them. The biscuits were a light tan colour and, after seeing Julie eating one, we decided on the name Rusk, which seemed very appropriate as she was the same colour as the biscuit.

A Lakeland terrier's hair, as it grows, has to be stripped at regular intervals to prevent it from getting too long and matted. After being stripped they look like matchstick dogs. By the time Rusk was six months old she needed to be stripped for the first time. This would be a regular four to six-monthly job (in our household six-monthly, as it was quite expensive) and I was pleased that we were able to take her back to the breeder to do the job. In order for her to keep her wiry hair, she needed to be stripped and not clipped, and I knew the breeder would not make that mistake.

The first time we had Rusk stripped we brought home our very own matchstick dog. She looked like she would be at home in any Lowry painting. Chris and the children became very adept at drawing square-muzzled, stick-legged cartoon dogs that looked just like her. The following comment by a passer-by one day seemed to say it all, "I had a dog like that when I was a child but it had a handle and four wheels."

Rusk was a true family dog and was fun. Just what

we wanted. As a pup she did make a few mistakes, like chewing through the telephone cable (well, fancy putting it along the bottom sill of the back door) and shredding a small chair when I popped in to see the next-door neighbour for five minutes. She was obviously a bit cross about that, but these were small errors and soon forgiven. Her zest for life and friendly nature soon meant she had won over everyone.

When Rusk was young there was an appeal on the TV programme *Blue Peter* for people to puppy-walk for Guide Dogs for the Blind. This involved having a puppy for a year and teaching it to be a confident, well-behaved dog. I couldn't get excited about doing that. The thought of having a puppy every year to house-train, teach basic obedience and socialise, and at the same time take the risk of having more chairs chewed, was not my idea of fun. Ten years later, I was going to have to eat my words.

Rusk loved to play with a ball – not a tennis ball but a large football. She would dribble it around the lawn at great speed, using her muzzle to control and propel it, either on her own or with one of the children challenging her. She was hard to catch and negotiated obstacles and corners at lightning speed. Many a professional footballer would have been pleased to have her dribbling skills. It was quite a sight to see this small dog moving adeptly around the garden at such a pace, moving a ball that was bigger than her head.

Rusk playing football

When Rusk was about twelve months old and had had her first season, it was time for her to be spayed. She went into the vets to be operated on and when she returned would have to be kept quiet for ten days until her stitches were removed. She was very quiet when she came back from the vet as she was still recovering from the anaesthetic. We made her a cosy bed by the radiator and she became a pampered pet that evening. I was lulled into a false sense of security as it looked as though it was going to be quite easy to achieve the task of keeping her quiet.

At the time we had a large concrete coal bunker in the back garden, the sort with a lift-up lid at the top and a pop-hole opening at the front where the coal would trickle out, and a spade could be used to dig it out and into the coal bucket. As Rusk had to be kept quiet for her recovery we needed to stop her playing football and had popped the ball into the top of the coal bunker out of her way. The next morning as I came downstairs into the kitchen I heard Chris in the back garden shouting at her. *How could he be so mean to her?* I thought, as she was still recovering from her operation. I went outside to discover the reason for all the noise. Rusk had recovered from her anaesthetic and was busy dragging herself on her newly stitched tummy through the pop hole, over the bits of shiny black coal and into the coal bunker in a very determined effort to get to her ball. She was obviously feeling much better and didn't realise the importance of not pulling out her stitches. No harm was done, but trying to keep her quiet for ten days was obviously going to be more difficult than we had initially thought.

At the time we lived in a semi on a large corner plot with a concrete patio across the width of the house at the back and raised beds containing roses bordering it. This area was covered by a car port (in this case a large corrugated plastic roof supported by a metal frame and a series of metal poles). There was a path in the centre of the beds that led out onto a large lawn bordered by a variety of shrubs and bushes. Two-thirds of the way down the garden there was a shed on the left-hand side next to our newly erected six-foot fence, and next to that were three apple trees, two producing pounds of cooking apples each year and one producing eating apples. Beyond that was the vegetable patch and a cherry tree. In contrast to the apple trees the cherries were always stolen by the birds before we got to harvest them, and I soon understood why cherries were always so expensive in the shops. We were often out in the garden trying to keep on top of things, and whenever we were out there Rusk was with us with her football. Whatever we were doing – digging, weeding, mowing the lawn – she was there, ever hopeful that someone would kick it for her.

One day, this obsession with the ball nearly had disastrous consequences. Chris was clearing a rough area at the end of the garden and needed a pickaxe to get out an old tree stump. As the pickaxe came down, Rusk rushed in head first with her ball. There was no chance of either stopping, and the two met at ground level. There were desperate yelps from Rusk and two panic-stricken pet owners. She ran indoors and hid behind the settee in the lounge. I went to see what damage had been done. She was shaking like a leaf, but apart from that she seemed OK. I phoned the vet for advice. He said to check that her eyes weren't rolling or doing anything strange and just keep an eye on her. She was very quiet for about two hours and stayed behind the settee. Then, being a tough little terrier, she emerged from her refuge and ventured out into the garden… to play ball. That evening there were two very relieved pet owners.

At times Rusk tended to live life on a knife-edge. One warm summer evening while I was sitting indoors with the patio doors open, enjoying the late evening sunshine, Rusk came and lay on the floor by my feet. I put my hand down and started to stroke her. As I did so, I noticed that she had lots of little lumps in her hair which I thought were some seed heads that she had picked up whilst playing outside. At the time Rusk's hair was long and woolly, just at the point where she would need to be stripped, which was probably lucky, as when I investigated the lumps they weren't seed heads as I'd anticipated but wasps, and they were still alive. She had probably pushed her football into the wasps' nest that was in the ground by the biggest apple tree. As her hair was so long and curly at the time, the wasps hadn't managed to get through it to sting her body. I then had the challenge of getting them out without getting stung myself. I used a comb to carefully pull through her coat and remove the offending wasps one at a time. Rusk lay there and let me work at the coat for an hour, without moving or complaining, making my job much better than it could have been. We were both lucky to escape unscathed, and I removed over thirty wasps from her coat. The wasps' nest at the base of the apple tree was very quickly dealt with and no harm came to anyone.

Caravanning in Charmouth in Dorset was Rusk's first introduction to family holidays. We stayed in a large static caravan on a holiday park, a short walk downhill to the beach. We had dog-loving friends staying in an identical caravan next door who had children slightly older than ours. A beach and a football were Rusk's idea of heaven. Add to that a whippet who came to the beach for the day and fancied a good run and she was on cloud nine. The two dogs ran up and down the long sandy beach for most of the day. She certainly slept well that evening. On the beach the next day we met the whippet again. This time Rusk declined his invitation to have a run. She had obviously not paced herself the previous day and had a few aching muscles, which needed time to recover.

Chris has always been a canal enthusiast. For many summers we holidayed on a canal boat and these holidays also included Rusk. She was happy to ride on the boat or walk with us on the towpath. Being a small dog she fitted neatly in the narrow gangway and would curl up on the floor by one of the beds at night. She was happy to sit up at the bow of the boat watching the world go by and then trot along to the noisier back of the boat and sit with the driver. No footballs were allowed on these holidays, though. Rusk's first mistake on a canal was to confuse grass and duckweed. Whilst running along the towpath with us one day she suddenly decided to head off and have a run around on a large area of green that she could see ahead, blissfully unaware that it was duckweed and not grass. At full speed, she ran off the towpath into an area of canal covered in duckweed and landed with a loud splash right in the middle of the canal. Her excellent swimming skills came into their own; she surfaced looking a little surprised but none the worse for her misadventure. We, on the other hand, had a very wet, green dog to deal with. Washing down a dog with the facilities available on a canal boat is not the easiest of tasks, and everyone was hoping that she wouldn't choose their bed to sleep next to that night.

One of the things we love about canal boat holidays is operating the locks which enable the boat to go up or downhill. Most of the time, Rusk walked along the towpath with the members of the crew who were working the locks. Usually locks come in ones or twos and are interspersed with long periods of walking along the towpath. Those walking on the towpath could wait at the next bridge to hop back on the boat when they had had their fill of walking, and Rusk was no exception. Sometimes there are flights of locks where the locks come in quick succession. One day we were travelling down a long flight and Rusk as usual got off the boat to walk along the towpath with us. We worked them very efficiently and by 4pm had reached the end of the flight. When we looked around there was no sign of Rusk. We were trying to remember where we had last seen her, and retraced our steps, hoping against hope that she hadn't fallen into the canal or got caught in one of the locks and drowned when we weren't looking. It wasn't long before we found her about three locks back, fast asleep on the grassy bank. We woke her up and she followed us back to the boat. She got on and lay down at the back by the tiller, with her head just hanging over the edge of the boat looking at the water. This was to be her position for the next couple of days. Again, she had failed to pace herself.

After four years of Rusk being an only dog, we gained two more pets – two six-week-old guinea pigs. One was a golden colour and the other was black. By this time we had had our second child Mark, and so the two children would have a guinea pig each to look after – under my supervision. The idea was to teach them to care for their own animal, and guinea pigs seemed an ideal choice. They were a good-sized pet for the children to handle. They didn't bite, and also they responded to people with a high-pitched squeak, which the children learnt to imitate and used to have 'conversations' with their pets. Julie's guinea pig was the golden one and she called her Honey. Mark, who was three years old at the time, called his Gumdrop after the old black car in his favourite storybook.

There was great excitement the day the guinea

pigs arrived. They were brought into the kitchen in a large cardboard box full of straw. The children sat on the floor in the kitchen with newspaper on their laps, to mop up any guinea pig accidents, and one at a time had turns at holding and stroking them. I was one very anxious mother as I reminded them again and again to be gentle, trying to prevent any escapees whilst itching to have a cuddle myself.

In the summer we kept the hutch on the lawn with an enclosed run attached to it. We regularly moved the hutch and the run around the lawn to prevent the lawn going yellow, and to give the guinea pigs new, fresh grass to eat. Guinea pigs are particularly good at keeping the grass 'mown'. Unlike rabbits, they don't dig, so they don't leave any holes in the lawn. We always felt that if we had enough guinea pigs and let them all free run, we wouldn't need to do any mowing at all, but as we had a big lawn we would have needed a lot of them.

In the winter we kept the hutch on a table at the sheltered end of the patio and covered it with a thick blanket at night, but in really cold weather we put the hutch in the garage at the side of the house. Guinea pigs are prone to chest infections and so need to be protected from really bad winter weather.

Both Honey and Gumdrop were very tame and enjoyed being held, sitting on our laps and eating treats such as carrots, cabbage and apples. When

Gumdrop and Marmalade

they were in their hutch and we put the treats in the run, Gumdrop was always the first to come and get something and then take it back home to eat. However, Honey always took it from her, and so Gumdrop had to venture out again to get something for herself. Honey was definitely the boss and often sent Gumdrop out to do the work then enjoyed the rewards herself.

One day, when they were about three years old, we went out to deal with the animals as usual in the evening only to discover that they were having a great deal of trouble breathing. It looked like both guinea pigs were ill with bronchitis or pneumonia; Honey in particular looked very poorly, and so we made an appointment to see the vet the next day.

Their breathing sounded very gravelly and we put them in cardboard boxes lined with a bed of straw and brought them indoors to keep them warm in the lounge overnight. Sadly, Honey died during the morning, before we could take her to the vet. Gumdrop, however, survived to make it to the vet's and after a course of antibiotics was just as fit as ever. A few months later we got another guinea pig for Julie. This one was a dark ginger colour with a white flash on her nose and she called her Marmalade, often nicknamed Sticky Marmalade. Gumdrop, in the meantime, was getting more confident and one day, while in the winter quarters, rushed out when the hutch door was opened and fell about three feet onto the concrete floor below. The poor thing couldn't move, so we picked her up carefully and went to the vet. Things didn't look very hopeful as it looked as though she may have broken her back. The vet examined Gumdrop, gave her a steroid injection and said, "Come back in a couple of days." I could read between the lines that her chances of recovery were slim but, because Julie and Mark were there, nothing was said outright. Much to the vet's surprise, we made our return visit two days later with a guinea pig that was showing some signs of recovery. With more treatment and time, about four weeks, Gumdrop made a full recovery and was once again living life to the full. After that we were always very careful to have our hands ready to catch any animal that might be ready to fall out of the hutch.

Rusk was used to having the guinea pigs around and, although she was a terrier, took no notice of them. It was a different matter when friends visited with their rescue dog, Magee. She was a small, smooth-haired, black dog with some white areas around her face. She couldn't take her eyes off the guinea pigs and we had to be extra vigilant when she came to stay. We even moved them into the garage sometimes when she came, to give them some peace and quiet.

Sadly, one day when the guinea pigs were out in their run on the lawn, Magee found a small hole in the side of the run and she caught Sticky Marmalade and that was the end of her. Julie was away on a school visit at the time and I wasn't looking forward to telling her about the demise of Marmalade when she got back. Gumdrop, ever the survivor, managed to keep well away from trouble that day and lived happily until she was seven and a half years old, a good age for a guinea pig.

Frankie, my first guide dog puppy

Rusk was just like another member of the family. We took her everywhere with us on days out, and holidays were always planned around being able to take Rusk with us. She never seemed to age, although when she was nearly ten years old she often limped or held her right hind leg up, but it still didn't stop her playing her beloved football. Several months later she hurt her left hind leg. Playing football on three legs hadn't been a problem for her, but when both hind legs hurt it was a different matter. The vet examined her under a general anaesthetic and phoned me to say that unfortunately he couldn't do anything for her. I made what I felt was a rational, instant decision there and then that the kindest thing for her was to have her put to sleep. She wouldn't have enjoyed life without going for walks and being able to play football. Looking back, I think she must have damaged her cruciate ligament. These days she could have had an operation to cure the problem, but over thirty-five years ago it wasn't an option.

I had kept cool and calm whilst I was talking on the telephone, but as soon as I put the receiver down on the handset I burst into tears. I went and sat on the bottom of the stairs to have a good cry on my own, but I was joined very quickly by our youngest child, three-year-old David, who was also in tears. "Why are you crying, Mummy?" he asked. I tactfully skirted round this question by asking him the same thing. He replied, "Because you are crying." So we both sat at the bottom of the stairs having a cuddle and a good cry. Well, it's the best thing to do at a time like that.

Our house was a very sad place after she had died. Going out into the garden and finding a favourite ball of hers when I was gardening was enough to set me off crying, and the space in the kitchen where her bed used to be felt very empty indeed. Rusk died in 1982 aged ten years old, not very old for a dog, particularly a terrier. At the time, Julie was eleven years old, Mark eight and David three. We were all very sad that we didn't have Rusk anymore. We all missed having a lively dog under our feet, playing around in the garden with us and going on daily walks, but decided not to have another dog as we were all so upset when she died. We would have to make do with talking to other people's dogs instead.

A couple of months after this I met a neighbour walking a lively, ten-week-old yellow Labrador puppy. He was called Lucas. I couldn't resist having a pat and a cuddle but I did ask if he wasn't a bit young to be out walking the streets. "He's a guide dog puppy," was the reply from Muriel. "They have their initial vaccinations when they're about six weeks old so that they can go out into the big wide world and get used to as many different sights and sounds as possible at an early age. I'm puppy walking him. We keep the puppy until it is about one, then it goes to one of the Guide Dogs Centres for training." Muriel was obviously really enjoying her new puppy. *Interesting*, I thought. *A dog for a year that would still be alive when it went and, after some more training, would be a guide and companion for a blind person.* I had forgotten that ten years earlier I had ruled out the idea of puppy-walking because of the thought of all the damage they could do and the effort that went into house-training and teaching basic obedience. Rusk's misdemeanours as a young puppy and the effort that went into training her were now so long ago they were a distant memory, but the effect of her dying had had a much stronger impact on me. A dog that hadn't died when it left you was a definite bonus. It made having a dog a real possibility again. A large, moulting Labrador didn't meet our other specifications though; we wanted a small dog that didn't moult; but I was obviously missing a dog about the house so much that I was prepared to waive some of my original requirements.

That evening as I prepared our dinner I contemplated how I would broach the subject with the family. They too would be happy to have a dog that wasn't going to die, and I was sure they could be tempted by a cute little puppy. They had been so young when Rusk arrived, none of them remembered her as a young dog, and I knew they were finding family life without a dog to share it with as incomplete as I was. Once dinner was served and everyone was happily tucking in, I put the idea of puppy-walking to the family. "I met Muriel Fry this morning. She was out walking a very young Labrador puppy. It turns out that she is puppy-walking it for Guide Dogs for the Blind." That got everyone's interest, and I was soon sharing all the details that I had gleaned from Muriel with them. After that there was nothing left but to put my suggestion to them. I took a deep breath and went for it. "I was wondering if it was something we might be able to do? What do you think?" There was an animated discussion about the matter and then we took a vote on it. The result was four to one in favour. Mark was the one who was not too excited about it but, as I was going for a majority decision, I began to make enquiries at the Wokingham Guide Dogs Centre about puppy-walking.

A few weeks after our family discussion and subsequent phone call to Guide Dogs, I was visited by a puppy-walking supervisor. This is the first step for any potential new puppy-walker and was effectively my interview for the job. I was keen to make a good impression and had made sure the house was clean and tidy for her visit and ready for the occasion. Julie and Mark were at school and David was at playgroup, so I had nothing to distract me from the job in hand, which was important as I knew I was going to be feeling nervous. The supervisor was held up on her way to us which didn't help my nerves, and it was a long wait before the Guide Dog van eventually turned into the drive and a young lady stepped out of it. She was wearing blue jeans and a Guide Dog top and I felt slightly overdressed in my skirt. I was soon to learn that jeans were the preferred attire of most Guide Dog staff and that soon I too would be wearing them on a daily basis – the perfect dog-training wear.

I opened the door to greet her. "Monica Easton? I'm Sara, the puppy-walking supervisor from Guide Dogs. I'm so sorry I'm later than I said." I invited her in and we were soon chatting away easily over a cup of tea and a biscuit. There were certain criteria that we needed to fulfil to be considered for puppy-walking. First of all, she checked that I was at home most of the day and would not be leaving the puppy alone for long periods of time. Then the garden was checked to make sure it was dog-proof. The six-foot fencing was still in place and doing its job well, so we had passed all the basic requirements.

The fact that we had already owned a dog meant that I understood something about how they behaved and would interact with the family, which also helped. She then gave me an idea of what would be expected of me, and some basic training in how to puppy-walk. She explained all the dos and don'ts of the job. Training begins at day one. Some of the basic commands for puppy and me to learn were 'sit', 'wait', 'down', 'stay', 'come', 'leave', 'eat' and 'busy' (the magic word to encourage the puppy to go to the toilet). Although I would be doing it as a volunteer and would not be paid, Guide Dogs would cover the cost of the food, and all the vet's fees would be paid.

My situation met all the requirements and I was still enthusiastic to have a puppy, so my name was put on the waiting list. I was going to be accepted as a puppy-walker. I knew I was going to get a big dog that would moult, I knew that the dog would have to be good with children, so my only request left was for a bitch. At dinner that night I had some good news to share with the family and they were as excited as I was.

There was a shortage of puppies at the time and so we had to wait. It felt like a very long five months before I got a phone call from Sara to say a pup was available. A litter of seven Labrador cross golden retriever puppies had been born. There were two bitches and five dogs; the bitches had been allocated to previous walkers so would I consider having one of the dogs? Would I like to think about it and let her know? It was all I could do not to abandon our final requirement on the spot and just say "Yes" straight away.

As soon as Chris got home from work I discussed it with him. Having waited such a long time to be offered a guide dog pup to walk we were very willing to consider having a dog instead of a bitch. It would only be for a year – not the same as buying a puppy as a pet, which we would have for ten years or more – and we could always have a bitch the next time, so half an hour later I phoned back to say we would have a dog.

Sara was very pleased, but it wasn't until later that I discovered more puppy-walkers asked for bitches and it was more difficult to place the dogs. Straight away she gave us his details. He was a golden retriever crossed with a Labrador and his name was Frankie. His father was called Toffee (the golden retriever) and his mother was the Labrador called Imogen. He was born on 2nd April and would come to us on 18th May, in about four weeks' time. We had to supply his bed, blankets and bowls, and Guide Dogs would provide collars, leads, identity discs, powdered milk, food and pay any vet's fees we incurred. "I'll see you with Frankie on 18th May, then," said Sara. We concluded our conversation and I put the phone down. I was very excited.

There were a few things to do to be ready for Frankie's arrival, and I set about the preparations with enthusiasm helped by an equally enthusiastic family. Rusk's bed was a wicker basket made by a blind person. As a pup she chewed the edges quite a lot, so we decided to start Frankie off with a sturdy cardboard box from the local supermarket. We cut an opening on the long side, wrote his name on it in black marker pen and put an old blanket in it. We bought a blue non-tip plastic dog bowl, a packet of breakfast cereal, some dog meat and mixer biscuits, and then waited for 18th May. It was one of the longest four weeks I have known.

Eventually May 18th came and our much-anticipated pup arrived. Sara left him in the van at first so that we could do the paperwork without being distracted, although I still found it hard to concentrate on it knowing that Frankie was just outside. Then we went to get Frankie. He came to the open door of the van quite confidently, a good sign apparently. He was a lovely tan colour and a very handsome pup. We took him straight out into the garden to go to the toilet. It was our first chance to use our newly acquired guide dog language. "Busy," I said hopefully as he wandered around the lawn. 'Busy' is the key word that is used by Guide Dogs to let the dog know that you want them to go to the toilet. Neither we nor Frankie were familiar with the term but we used it enthusiastically and were rewarded with him going to the toilet 'on command'. Much praise and encouragement was showered on Frankie, who enjoyed the fuss, but it would be some time before he fully understood the term. This was my first introduction to the command 'Busy', a word that was to be used many, many times in my life. Sara left us soon after that, and I was suddenly aware of the responsibility I had been given in looking after someone else's very valuable dog. My lifetime as a puppy-walker had begun.

Until Frankie was house-trained we wanted to keep him in the kitchen, so Chris had cut a piece of wood that was about knee high and would just fit into the door frame from the kitchen to the dining room. It was high enough to stop the puppy, but still allowed the family to get over. This included David who was four years old at the time. As we were great canal enthusiasts, this piece of wood was always known as the stop-plank. On canals, stop-planks are pieces of wood that are used to block off a section of the canal so it can be drained and maintenance carried out. We had the stop-plank all ready for Frankie's arrival. We knew all the family could get over it but hadn't tested it on any real live dogs. The day that Frankie arrived, my parents came to see him and brought their eight-month-old cairn terrier, Lyn. She came in very excitedly, rushed down the hall, through the dining room and easily jumped over the stop-plank to get into the kitchen. Perhaps we would have to re-think the height of the stop-plank; if an eight-month-old cairn terrier could jump it what use would it be with a dog the size of a Labrador? It turned out that, although bigger than spry little Lyn, Frankie was floppier and less jumpy. It was a few months before he was co-ordinated enough to jump the stop-plank, by which time we had got the very battered stairgate down from the loft and used that to separate the dog from the rest of the house when we needed to – usually when he was drying off after a particularly muddy walk.

As Frankie was only going to be with us for a year I had decided not to get too attached to him. I would follow all the Guide Dog rules but remain slightly distant from him. A good idea, but Frankie was a clever dog and decided to play me at my own game. If I wasn't going to love him dearly, there was no way he was going to co-operate with my wishes. So I reluctantly gave in and quickly became very fond of my charge.

Frankie still played hard to get and refused to walk on a lead anywhere willingly until he was twelve weeks old. It would take me half an hour to walk him about fifty yards. I used all the tricks of the Guide Dog trade – a coaxing voice, dangling keys or a toy in front of him, or getting one of the family to walk ahead of us – but to no avail. He would lay flat on his tummy, with his front legs forward, his hind legs backwards, and would refuse to move. We referred to this position as the Frankie flop. He was not frightened, but just exhibiting the retriever stubbornness in his breeding.

The Frankie flop

Being a first-time puppy-walker I had very little experience to draw on and was flummoxed by this dog who refused to walk. I rang my supervisor. "He just won't walk. We've tried everything and all he does is lie down on the floor and refuse to move. What should I do?" Sara arranged for an extra support visit for me from Matt, one of the trainers at the Wokingham training centre. We settled ourselves in the lounge to discuss my problems with Frankie. It wasn't long before Frankie decided to sit next to Matt and even ease his way gently onto his lap. I had sat on the floor with Frankie on my lap, but not when I was relaxing in an armchair, and I had thought this behaviour was against Guide Dog rules. He gently stroked Frankie's head saying, "It isn't really fair on Frankie that I will be taking him for a walk as he doesn't really know me." From where I was sitting I couldn't see that there was any problem at all.

After nearly an hour of this bonding we went out for a walk along the pavements in Charvil. Matt walked Frankie on a lead by his left-hand side. I followed behind to watch and learn. Frankie walked perfectly. No pulling, no Frankie flops, just the perfect demo of how it should be done. I was a bit deflated, as Frankie was just about four months old and I had never managed such a good walk. Matt did give me some encouragement, though. "If a young pup doesn't want to walk it can experience lots of sights and sounds by being carried and at the same time feel safe and secure. By the time they are too heavy to be carried, they will probably want to walk anyway." He related this to walking with a toddler or young child and picking them up and carrying them if they were tired and reluctant to walk.

I found this advice really useful for the rest of my puppy-walking years. A trip to the local post office and back for future puppies was a little walk and then a little carry. I was a cross between a puppy-carrier and a puppy-walker. It wasn't until he was about five months old that Frankie finally decided that walking could be fun.

All was going well until Frankie was nearly six months old and he was introduced to family holidays. We went on holiday to an old cottage in Herefordshire for a fortnight. Mark was a really active child who loved the outdoors, and we loved walking, so a holiday in the Shropshire hills with plenty of places to explore and fun walks for the dog seemed to be an ideal choice. Our Maxi car was full to the brim with things for the dog, the children and us, and we had had to invest in an aluminium roof rack for extra luggage. The journey took about three hours and Frankie spent it travelling in the well of the passenger seat. He was a good traveller and the journey passed quickly. Once we got there Frankie decided that holidays were not for him and no way was he going to walk. We quickly went back to the Frankie flop stage for the whole of the first week of that holiday. So much for choosing a holiday that you think the dog will enjoy.

This was not to be our only problem on that memorable holiday. On the first night at the cottage, as I settled down on the sofa ready to relax for the evening, I started stroking Frankie. As I rubbed him around the neck area I noticed several small lumps. I was reminded of Rusk's incident with the wasps and decided I should investigate further. As I gently lifted Frankie's hair up and back, I discovered about twelve abscesses on his chest, some big, some small, so the next day a trip to the vet was called for.

I hadn't anticipated a sick dog on holiday, especially one that wasn't mine but one that I was responsible for. I had to telephone the Guide Dogs Centre and ask for their advice. The nearest red-painted public phone box was just down the road (there were no mobile phones at that time). It was the old-fashioned style where you lifted the receiver, dialled the number that you wanted, put money into the box section and when someone answered the phone you pressed button 'A' and you were connected. "Guide Dogs." That was the reply I wanted. "I'm Frankie's puppy-walker, we're on holiday and he's covered with numerous abscesses on his chest. What should I do?"

"Take him to a vet, get a receipt for the cost of the treatment and we will refund you the money when you get back home." I was glad it was a short phone call as long-distance daytime telephone calls at the time were quite expensive.

Our cottage was part of a smallholding and the owner gave us the contact details of the vet that they used. We found the surgery and got an appointment straight away. The vet lanced the biggest abscesses and we had to go back every day for the next three days to have them checked. By that time the smaller ones had gone down and those he had treated were healing well. Unfortunately, these were not to be our only visits to the vets that holiday.

By the start of our second week on the holiday, Frankie's abscesses were better and he had decided to walk again. In fact, he found it was fantastic fun free running in the country. On one of his free runs, he even managed to find the remainder of someone's sandwich in an old polythene bag. We tried to get it away from him, but he was determined to keep his loot and swallowed it quickly. As it turned out in the end, this was not a good move. We continued our walk and Frankie drank water from several streams. After a while we could see that his stomach was swelling up and bloating out. He was not feeling at all well, so Chris and I took it in turns to carry him for the rest of the walk until we got to the car. It is amazing how heavy a five-month-old puppy can be when you are having to carry him.

While we were carrying him, we could hear a sloshing, slopping sound. "Can you hear that sound in his stomach?" I asked as we were carrying him. The children were very worried and interested and came to have a listen too. After a while we realised that it was the water slopping around in his stomach. The polythene bag must have blocked some part of his intestine and was preventing the water that he had drunk earlier from passing through his system.

We went back to the vet again that evening and again the next day. He agreed that it was probably a blockage stopping the water going down into the intestine and that the most likely culprit was the polythene bag that he had scavenged earlier that day. We needed to watch Frankie carefully and take him back the following day. We should keep a close eye on his toileting. If the bag came out naturally he would be fine but, if not, then Frankie would need to have surgery to remove it. I telephoned Guide Dogs to report this latest emergency and we watched his toileting with a keen and hopeful eye for the next twenty-four hours, with three very helpful children rushing out into the cottage garden every time the dog did. Thankfully the bag did come out naturally and he survived that episode without the need for surgery, but we decided at that point we were never going to take a puppy on holiday with us again. Seven trips to the vet on a two-week holiday was not our idea of fun.

As puppy-walkers, we are expected to introduce our pups to as many different situations as possible so they will be confident and able to cope with all that they will meet when eventually working with a blind owner. Traffic and general noise didn't worry Frankie, but public transport and going into telephone boxes made him rebel again. It became quite an issue and one that was becoming very hard to win. We went out on special walks just to practise going into telephone boxes, but Frankie had no intention of going into one. I could go in if I liked but he would wait outside. Not to be beaten, I tried to entice him in with small pieces of cheese, but to no avail. In the end I enlisted the help of my puppy-walking supervisor who had no more luck than I had had. In the end, in desperation, she eventually pushed him in, hoping that she hadn't ruined him for life. She hadn't. In fact, after that he wanted to go into every telephone box that we passed. Perhaps it is significant that his eventual Guide Dog owner worked as a telephone switchboard operator.

Frankie's dislike of public transport also had to be conquered. He was always reluctant to get into the supervisor's van but his main problem was buses. To try and conquer this, Chris and I took Frankie and a pocketful of small pieces of cheddar cheese to Reading bus station one Sunday afternoon. The bus station was in a large, concrete area underneath a block of shops. The buses were lined up at the bus stops and it was generally a bleak and noisy place to be – not my first choice for a Sunday afternoon's entertainment. The staff we met were sympathetic to our problem and happy to help. We showed them the puppy-walker identification badge that all puppy-walkers are given and asked if there was a bus that wasn't going anywhere that we could use to try and get our Guide Dog puppy on board. We were shown a suitable vehicle to practise on and eventually he got on and off a bus, first of all using the cheese and eventually without any bribing at all. We must have been a strange sight, two people cajoling and talking to a dog trying to get him on and off a bus. In the end, like the telephone box, we had done such a good job that from then on Frankie always wanted to get on any bus that stopped near us when we were walking.

Frankie would not have been an easy dog for even an experienced walker, but for a first-timer he was especially challenging. I had had my work cut out training him and between us we had overcome many problems but, by the time he was a year old and ready to go in for training, Frankie was showing all the signs of becoming an excellent guide dog. He was confident and unfazed by unusual things around him and was a pleasure to take for a walk; and, in spite of my best efforts not to, I had become very attached to him.

It was time for him to go to the Wokingham Training Centre, but with his stubborn nature coming to the fore he was not going to go without a protest. When Sara came to collect him he decided he didn't want to go and did a Frankie flop on the doorstep. When he was a small puppy it was possible to pick him up and carry on. Now, as a seventy-pound adult dog, this was not a possibility, and much as he wanted to stay he really did need to go. To help with the situation I used my most encouraging voice to get him to the van. He got in reluctantly, my supervisor said goodbye and drove off, and I went back indoors to do the washing up. Half the water in the bowl must have been my tears. He didn't want to leave us and I didn't want him to go. Perhaps puppy-walking wasn't going to be the easy answer to having a dog that I thought it would be, but at least he was still alive.

Little did I know it at the time, but that was definitely not the last I was to see of Frankie. About nine months after Frankie left us, Julie hurt her arm and we went to the Royal Berkshire Hospital in Reading to have it X-rayed. We had parked the car in an on-road free parking space on the perimeter of the hospital, which was more convenient and easier to use than the car park. When we got back to the car there was a Guide Dog van parked opposite our car with several blind students, trainee guide dogs and guide dog trainers. I recognised one of the trainers as Frankie's trainer. "Oh, look," I said to Julie. "There's Frankie's trainer in that Guide Dog van. I wonder if Frankie is out training today? I could go and say hello." This was a good distraction from the broken arm, and I needed very little encouragement from Julie to go over and introduce myself. I had spoken to Frankie's trainer a couple of months earlier at the training centre and she had said that if I saw her out with Frankie I could speak to her and also see my pup. I crossed the road and asked if Frankie was there. When she realised I was his puppy-walker she said, "Yes, he's here," and pointed to the dog and Guide Dog owner standing next to her. I was introduced to Ian, and when Frankie recognised me he switched from being a responsible guide dog to an excited 'brain gone to jelly' animal.

We chatted for a few minutes and, during the conversation, I discovered that Ian worked in Reading, and he invited me to visit him sometime when I was in town. I took him up on this offer several months later and discovered that, after our first meeting when they were in training, Frankie hadn't worked very well for the rest of the day as he kept looking over his shoulder to see if we were following. These two meetings with Ian were to be the beginning of a friendship that continues to this day. I was able to see Ian and Frankie working together as a team many times after that and was always impressed with the way that Frankie would guide Ian around the many obstacles that he came across on his way to and from the office in the centre of town.

The following poem was written by Muriel & Tom Fry who set me off on my puppy-walking career. Suzy, their second puppy, was Frankie's contemporary.

Frankie

Dear Frankie, we loved you
We thought you were great,
But now you must leave us,
Don't get in a state.

You'll meet lots of doggies
All working quite hard,
We hope you'll see Suzy
In the exercise yard.

If you see her, please tell her
We miss her a lot,
And we'll love her forever,
Be she clever or not.

So, Frankie, be happy
Whatever you do,
Remember we love you
And the Eastons do too.

By Tom and Muriel Fry

Gerbils and Hamster

Of all our children, David, our youngest, was the one who most shared my love of animals. Being the youngest, we already had a dog and Julie and Mark's pet guinea pigs in the family when he was born, but pet acquisition and care stepped up a notch once David was old enough to want pets of his own. David's first pets were gerbils. At different times Julie and Mark had brought home Pixie and Dixie, the pepper-coloured school gerbils, for the weekend, but David had made it his personal responsibility to look after them. So, for his fourth birthday we bought him two female gerbils. They were both black and a bit smaller than the school gerbils, with bright eyes and long tails, and were interested in everything.

Naming animals is always a subject of much discussion in our household and this time was no exception. David was given lots of interesting and unusual suggestions for different names for his gerbils, particularly by his sister, who I think was just a little disappointed when he decided to call them Pixie and Dixie. Not very original names, but it did show what an impression the school gerbils had made on him.

David loved Pixie and Dixie. They were quite lively animals, always on the move and very inquisitive but, although they didn't bite, they weren't very easy to handle. David was much better at that than me. He was relaxed with them and very patient. Each week when we cleaned out the cage we had to transfer Pixie and Dixie to a bucket, putting a wire mesh splatter guard weighted down on the top so that they didn't escape whilst we emptied out the sawdust from the tray at the bottom of the cage, washed it and then added clean sawdust. We always did this as quickly as possible as the two lively gerbils leapt around the bucket, keen to get back into their newly spruced home. When the time came to move them back, David would calmly put his hand into the bucket, scoop up one of the gerbils as it ran over his hand and cradle it gently until he could get it into the cage. I don't think he ever dropped one once and would just wait until the gerbil came to him. Gerbils have very sharp teeth and gnaw anything and everything around them. I was more concerned about the damage they could cause if they escaped, a state of mind which definitely hampered my gerbil-catching skills.

Even when Pixie and Dixie were safely in their cage, they managed to gnaw a hole in our floor-length curtains. Their cage lived on a low table in the living room, stationed next to a piece of wall between a window and the patio doors. One day, we made the mistake of putting the cage too close to the long, orange curtains that I had made for the patio doors. Somehow, the folds in the curtains had brushed against the bars of the gerbil cage and Pixie and Dixie had managed to chew a hole in one of the folds where it touched the cage. After that, I was very careful to make sure the cage and curtains were kept away from each other.

Pixie and Dixie lived until they were four years old, a good age for gerbils. David was upset when they died. He had been very responsible in how he looked after them and of the three children had spent the most time playing and building up a rapport with them. David really missed having a pet, and so Pixie and Dixie were soon replaced by one hamster.

David's birthday was in April, during the school Easter holidays, so we could go and choose his hamster on his birthday, which just happened to be a weekday. We found a pet shop that had three litters of hamsters for sale so we had plenty to choose from. The first litter we looked at were not friendly animals and were inclined to bite. The two other litters were very friendly and not at all hand-shy. David eventually selected the one he liked. I paid for the hamster and came home with a very excited birthday boy. David called him Dusty because he was a pale golden colour with greyish shades at the tips of his fur giving him a dusty appearance.

We all took turns to hold and stroke him. When it came to my turn I stroked him down the lie of the hair and then against it – this way I could check his skin, something I have a habit of doing with all furry animals. As I did it I noticed a couple of areas of eczema on his back. He would have to go back. I was not prepared to buy an animal that was not completely healthy.

Amidst much protesting from the children I put Dusty back in the box, bundled everyone into the car and drove back to the pet shop. The owner was very surprised to see us. I showed him the hamster and the patches of eczema. He suggested that I take Dusty to the vet surgery just along the road. Realising that I was not going to take up that option he offered David another one from that litter. I wasn't happy with that either, as all the litter were likely to be prone to the same problem, and I was not prepared to take on a potentially sick animal. Finally, we settled for a replacement hamster from the other friendly litter. Now satisfied customers,

Dusty the hamster

we came home with the replacement hamster that was a lovely deep golden colour, but was still going to be called Dusty. (Names are so difficult to choose.) He was perfectly healthy, quite a bit bigger than the gerbils and a much more placid animal to handle. Even I could pick him up without any worries.

David handled Dusty at every opportunity and would walk around with him in his shirt pocket. Many times he wandered into the kitchen to chat or ask a question, and I would turn round from making dinner to see a little furry face happily poking out and looking inquisitively at me. He would let him run free in his room, genuine free running, not in a hamster ball, and he made up short hurdle courses for him using his toy bricks. Dusty must have been a very fit animal. For added exercise, David would put the hamster on the bottom step of the stairs. Dusty would then climb the fourteen stairs, turn right at the top, and walk along the long narrow landing past Julie's room to David's room at the far end. The whole journey was timed by David on his stopwatch, with the recorded fastest time being nine seconds.

Dusty was the perfect pet... well, almost. Even he managed to get it wrong once. David had a brand new sweatshirt neatly folded in his chest of drawers. He went to get it out to wear one day and soon reappeared downstairs in the kitchen. "Mum, look at this." David held up the sweatshirt which had a hole halfway down the left sleeve and another halfway down the left side of the front, not really wearable in that state. During one of his free running sessions, Dusty had climbed into the back of the chest of drawers, chewed it and made himself a very cosy nest in the corner of the drawer.

As the sweatshirt was brand new I was reluctant to throw it out. I rummaged around in my sewing box and, after a little experimenting, managed to turn it into a designer item by stitching a one-inch wide piece of tape down the length of the sleeve and another length down the front from the shoulder to the bottom. The sweatshirt was wearable, looked much more 'trendy' than it had been originally, and Dusty was forgiven.

Gus and Errol,
chalk & cheese

Even though I had been very upset when Frankie had left, our first experience of puppy-walking had been a good one. I had learnt a lot about dog training, and the family had felt complete with a four-legged friend around, so I rang Sara my supervisor and said that I would like another puppy. Again I asked for a bitch. We were told that, if we didn't mind waiting, that would be fine but that we would get a puppy quicker if we would have a dog. It had seemed a very long wait until Frankie had arrived, so it didn't take long to make that decision; we said we would have another dog. We could always have a bitch next time. It was nearly three months after Frankie left us that our second puppy arrived. This time we had a pale yellow, pure Labrador pup called Gus. He had long lanky legs and big feet. Right from the beginning, everyone who met him took one look at his paws and said: "He's going to be a big dog; just look at the size of those paws." And they were right. It was with the advent of Gus that I began to learn how different the personalities of the dogs could be. Gus grew to be a gentle giant and was a laid-back animal, much more willing to please than Frankie and quite happy to walk anywhere and everywhere. I don't think he had a stubborn bone in his body, which took a bit of getting used to after Frankie.

Being a pure Labrador, Gus had a good appetite; even as a small pup of ten weeks he would quickly clear his food bowl, and he definitely didn't self-regulate his food intake. One evening I was going to be out at puppy feeding time, always a problem when your pup is on four meals a day. On this occasion I had asked Chris to feed him for the first time, which he was very happy to do. Having had a whole year of looking after Frankie we had a good system for keeping the dog food, and Chris knew exactly where everything was kept. What could possibly go wrong? I went out and had a very enjoyable evening at the local flower-arranging class.

I arrived home later on that evening and popped straight out to the kitchen to see how my new puppy was doing. He would probably need to 'busy' by now and I was keen to avoid an accident. I thought Gus looked quite quiet and very bloated, which wasn't his normal self. On the windowsill was his food bowl with some biscuits still in it, also very unusual. He normally licked his bowl so clean you had to look very closely to see whether it was dirty or not. My suspicions were aroused and so I asked Chris how much he had fed Gus. "One and a half pounds of meat and three-quarters of a pound of biscuits," was the reply – I gasped! This was the amount Frankie had been eating as a fully grown dog. The last time Chris had fed a dog was the full-grown Frankie, and I hadn't thought to tell him the amount to give our young puppy. This was quite a bit more than Gus should have had, as he was only eating four ounces of meat and two ounces of biscuits per meal at the time. No wonder he looked so bloated and uncomfortable. This was not a mistake I wanted to repeat, and ever since then I have written the quantity of food the dog is eating on a small sticker on the front of the food container so that whoever is feeding the dog can't make the same mistake.

Gus was a good pup, a natural guide dog and a pleasure to walk. He left us with many fond memories and very few funny stories as he always did the right thing. By the time he left I was beginning to feel confident in doing my job as a puppy-walker. He had done everything by the book, and all the training procedures used by Guide Dogs worked well for him. He left us at a year old to go to the Wokingham Training Centre and once again I shed tears. On entry into training I received a letter from Guide Dogs thanking me for all I had done for them in walking this puppy. (I received one of these letters for every dog I walked.) Even though Gus had been easy to train, I had spent many hours working with him, and I valued the written thanks that I received. I still have this, and the other letters, filed away in a special place. Gus was a qualified guide dog nine months later. He went to work with a lady in Kent who also rang to let me know how pleased she was with him. The photograph Guide Dogs sent of Gus with his owner joined my photograph of Frankie and Ian. For me this photograph is always an important reminder of what puppy-walking is all about, and an apt record of what each dog and owner have achieved.

Our next pup should have been a yellow Labrador called Troy, but a couple of weeks before he was due to arrive I had an urgent phone call from a member of Guide Dogs' staff at 3pm on a Friday afternoon. "Hello, Monica, I know you are expecting Troy in a couple of weeks but we have a bit of an emergency here and I wondered if you would mind a change.

Could you have a puppy straight away?" A first-time walker had arrived at the centre that afternoon with her ten-week-old Labrador puppy. She didn't want him anymore because he'd chewed the children's shoes, chewed the furniture and tiddled on the floor. "Oh," I said, "but they all do that."

Well, I was very happy to have him that day, but I was boarding Frankie for two weeks while his owner Ian was on holiday, and I was due to have my next guide dog puppy, Troy, in two weeks' time. "Not a problem," was the reply. "We just need to get him into a home straight away as he is far too young to put in the kennel block, and Troy will be placed with another puppy-walker." I quickly arranged for a friend to collect David from school, made sure the stop-plank was in place, got out the puppy bed, and was just about ready to receive this new puppy when he arrived. An hour later, I had another puppy to walk. Julie and Mark were very surprised when they arrived home from school to see the stop-plank in place and the puppy bed in the kitchen complete with a new puppy. I preferred puppies to arrive early in the day when the children were at school as it meant I could have a little time to settle them in quietly myself. Not so for this puppy who was called Errol. Not my first choice of a name for a dog, and it was several months before I could tell people his name without apologising for it and saying, "I didn't name him."

Errol as a pup

Errol had only been with us for twenty-four hours when I realised that his chewing and stealing was much worse than the average pup and perhaps his previous walker had had a point. His cardboard dog bed was already being destroyed, the old blanket that had been used as bedding for Frankie and Gus was being shredded and even the 'indestructible' dog toys were looking rather worse for wear. I was beginning to feel sorry for his previous walker. In his favour, Errol was a brilliant pup to walk. Nothing fazed him, and in no time at all we were working in very busy areas. Working guide dogs need to learn that when they are wearing the harness they are 'on duty', and Errol took to this concept really well as a pup, turning into a thoughtful, hard-working dog as soon as he was walking in just a collar and lead. Being distracted by stray food on the pavement was probably his only fault.

In contrast to this, the dogs also learn that when the harness comes off they are 'off duty'. Then they revert to being pets like any other dogs and Errol was no exception. When off the lead he had no qualms in breaking as many of the rules as he possibly could. He couldn't help it – it was the way he was made – and we couldn't help but love him.

When Errol was about five months old, yet another phone call came from Guide Dogs. A book publishing company was producing several books about working animals and one book was going to be about the training of guide dogs. They had followed one of the older dogs in training and now wanted to observe a puppy and its walker. Would I be prepared to do this? I felt very honoured to be asked and the thought of featuring in a book did rather go to my head. I said "Yes" straight away.

The following day, my supervisor and the two researchers for the book (one of whom was also the photographer) came to our house. I had plenty of tea, coffee, and biscuits for us to eat while we talked about Errol and puppy-walking. They had many questions, and with Errol being my third dog I was pleased that I could answer most of them, with my supervisor helping out on any others. With enough information gathered for the book we went into the garden and then on to Twyford for the photoshoot. I had decided to wear my green skirt as I preferred to be photographed in that rather than my, by now uniform, jeans.

Julie and Mark were not around that morning as they were at the local school swimming pool swimming five miles for one of the long-distance badges. David was not involved in the swimming and was much more enthusiastic to be around for the morning. He put on his favourite shorts and T-shirt just in case he might be in one of the photographs.

The dog in the book was to be called Danny. The previous day the team had photographed Cass, the dog who was going to be the adult Danny. Errol was being photographed as Danny the puppy. A comment was made by the researchers about how pale Errol was compared to Cass. In unison my supervisor and I replied: "They get darker as they get older," which is true, but I later learnt that Cass was a dark-coloured Labrador crossed with a golden retriever, and therefore much darker than Errol, who was a very pale Labrador and would never be the same shade as Cass; just a minor point really.

The photographer was keen to take some photos of Errol to illustrate some of the points of puppy-walking that we had been talking about. The first one was table manners. I pointed out at this stage that there could only be one take of this picture, and it would need to be quick as Errol ate fast, although with his true Labrador appetite would have loved to have had his meal several times over if they needed retakes. Errol sat very upright on the floor while I prepared him a small meal for photographic purposes. I put it on the floor a couple of feet in front of him. He waited until he heard me say, "Errol, eat!" then I blew one blast on the whistle. Within seconds the food was gone and the photograph successfully taken.

The second photograph was going to be taken outside in the garden. Guide dogs are trained to go to the toilet on command in a designated area of the garden. I wasn't sure this was the best photo for the book, and my supervisor and I tried hard to avoid it being taken. After his meal I quickly took Errol to an area at the end of the garden and used the command: "Busy boy!" hoping to beat the book researchers. They were too quick for me and the photographer grabbed her camera and rushed out after me. It must have been my lucky day as Errol went to the toilet straight away. Another 'one take' only photo that I had tried hard to avoid, but as it is a very important part of puppy-walking I suppose it was a 'must have' photo.

The next photographic session was in Twyford, a village a mile down the road from Charvil which has a small selection of shops on the roads leading up to the crossroads, and traffic lights in the centre. There was light rain to start with that day, so we needed waterproof coats at first, but the weather improved as the morning went on. We drove to Twyford and Errol travelled in the well of the passenger seat, which is where he would probably travel as a working guide dog so that was photographed too. We were beginning to get used to this stardom.

Walking through Twyford, Errol was distracted by a variety of things. Firstly, a large handsome dog, a German wirehaired pointer, walked past on a lead; then his next distraction was a grey-haired man in a long raincoat walking past us with a shopping bag full of food – how could he possibly not give that a good sniff? Once again Errol had provided the perfect photo opportunity. I encouraged him to ignore these things that could distract him as a working guide dog, whilst making sure he remained confident in the situation, as the photographer clicked away.

Several other photographs were taken in Twyford. One of my favourites was the one of Errol in the telephone box. Not all dogs are prepared to go into such a small space, as I had found out with Frankie, but this was not a problem for Errol. In fact, there was a pane of glass missing at the bottom of the old-fashioned box and so he popped his head out of it and watched the world go by. I love the photograph that she took of this.

Errol was confident in a busy situation like he experienced in Twyford. People were walking up and down the pavement, and cars and buses were passing close to him on the road, just what is needed in a guide dog. When I look back through photographs in the book I can see that the photographer managed to capture this perfectly.

We were photographed many times walking up and down the pavement; we were photographed many times in the telephone box; we were photographed many times outside the greengrocer's shop; and we were photographed many times outside the post office. At this point I realised that no way would I want to be a model or a film star. Errol, however, loved it and rose to the occasion. But eventually even he lay down on the pavement and protested. At this point the photography finished.

It was about two years later that I received my copy of the book *Guide Dog*. It was interesting to see our morning's work in print with many photographs, including Errol going to the toilet in the garden, which we had tried so hard to avoid being taken.

Errol was with us for another seven months, a challenging time for all. He was a real character who enjoyed breaking the rules and testing my patience as a puppy-walker. If the phone rang, I had to quickly move anything edible out of his reach before I picked up the receiver. If I didn't, it would disappear very quickly. We had to make sure our clothes were always put away; if not, he would take them and they would be much the worse for wear. Shoes and leather gloves were particular favourites, and Mark was very upset about the demise of his favourite shirt, which he had left lying around and Errol had found. The children all knew they needed to keep their things up out of Errol's way, so I was less sympathetic than I might have been. This was known in our house as 'the upping season', keeping everything up out of the puppy's way. With most puppies this was just a season, but with Errol it was for the whole year.

When friends came to stay one weekend I had baked some small cakes and scones. While my guard was down, Errol had taken the dozen cakes and shared them with Josie, a retired guide dog that we had adopted a few weeks earlier. Our next mistake was to forget to put the stair gate back after taking our friends' cases up the stairs. Errol went upstairs and found Auntie Pat's best fur hat. By the time we found him, the hat was looking much the worse for wear, never to be worn again. Thankfully Auntie Pat liked dogs and was very gracious about it, but I did feel very responsible for quite some time afterwards.

So life continued for the rest of Errol's stay with us. Cuddly toys were reduced to stuffing in half an hour. I had to keep tea towels and hand towels at the back of the kitchen work surfaces to stop him taking them. His bedding was ripped to pieces in a month, and we couldn't put any chocolates on the

Christmas tree or any boxes of them under it as he would help himself without a moment's hesitation. Chocolate is poisonous to dogs and we had to make sure he didn't get hold of it; even Errol with his cast-iron stomach needed to watch out for that.

Despite his bad ways, we all loved him. Julie said that if he were a human, she would compare him to Fletcher in the TV series *Porridge* – a loveable rogue. His redeeming feature was his willingness to work and to work well.

At a year old, Errol went into the Wokingham Guide Dogs Centre for further training. As he went I gave him a big cuddle and said, "Be a good dog, work hard and find yourself a good owner, but if you need a career change, you can come back." Did I really say that?

Errol did work hard at school, qualified quickly and went to work with a blind man in Sussex. Unfortunately, the partnership only lasted a few months as Errol proved to be too strong for his owner, who had a weak left arm, so it was back to school again for a refresher course. Then he re-trained with a man from Kent. Two puppy-walkers and then two owners; Errol was making a habit of this. The second partnership was much more successful and lasted until Errol was retired when he was eleven and a half years old – more about that later.

Errol's stay with us inspired the following:

She ♥s me –
She ♥s me not

I'm Errol – a Labrador puppy
She ♥s me

I have a good appetite
She ♥s me

I'm not aggressive
She ♥s me

I'm clean day and night
She ♥s me

I'm good when left in the house
She ♥s me

I picked a few flowers
She ♥s me not

I ate a wholemeal loaf
She ♥s me not

I tore her skirt
She ♥s me not

I had an accident on Auntie Pat's carpet!
She ♥s me not

I shredded a glove on her return!
She ♥s me not

I lay under the table at
meal times
She ❤s me

My basic obedience is
good
She ❤s me

My recall is excellent
She ❤s me

I'm well-behaved in
shops
She ❤s me

Nothing bothers me at
railway stations
She ❤s me

I was on my best
behaviour for the
supervisor's visit
She ❤s me

I chewed the leg of the
new chair
She ❤s me not

From the 'down' position
I can reach a height of six
feet at the mention of a
walk!
She ❤s me not

I arrive at top speed and
at head height!
She ❤s me not

I can open the back door
and let myself in
She ❤s me not

I ate too many stones and
had to go to the vet
She ❤s me not

I stole a dozen cakes to
celebrate
She ❤s me not

I can go up and down
stairs slowly
She ❤s me

I get on well with other
dogs
She ❤s me

I travel well on a bus
She ❤s me

I chewed Auntie Pat's
REAL fur hat!
She ❤s me not

I tore Mark's favourite
shirt
She ❤s me not

I stood on the table and
ate the Boss's dinner
She ❤s me not

In April 1986 the supervisor came to collect me.
As I limped away I heard, "You can
come back if you don't qualify!"
SHE ❤s ME!

By Monica Easton

Every year the resident dogs gave me a Christmas present accompanied by a poem written by Chris. This is the first of several which appear in this book:

To Missus

Missus, I am sorry
I chewed your slippers up;
It always is a worry
To be a lively pup.

I didn't mean to do it
But they were lying there;
You shouldn't tempt a fellow;
It really isn't fair.

To make up for the error
I sent the boss to town
With orders very thorough
To replace slippers, brown.

He made a valiant effort,
It didn't take him long,
So please accept replacement
And pardon my little wrong.

Luv Errol
(With some help from Chris Easton)

Josie joins the family

For the first time after our puppy went for training we were not dogless, a nice position to be in. When Errol was seven months old we had adopted Josie, a retired guide dog, but I'll leave her to tell her own story.

Just Josie

I'm Josie, a Labrador and a retired guide dog. I retired on 15th November 1985. It was a lovely sunny day at Folly Court, the Wokingham Guide Dogs Centre, when I left my guide dog owner to re-train with my successor – another Labrador called Zelda. I went to live with a puppy-walker in Charvil. I got into the back of her car – on the seat – she seemed to think I was going to travel on the floor. She soon realised there was little point in arguing with a 75lb Labrador.

I felt in pretty good condition for my age – eleven and a half years – occasional trouble with the anal gland, muscles in the back legs not all they used to be, and perhaps a few pounds overweight, but nothing to prevent me from enjoying my retirement. It was a good job I felt fit, as I had to share this retirement with a seven-month-old Labrador called Errol. He was a lively lad, but I soon had him under control. He was a thief if ever I saw one – we were going to get on well – a dog after my own heart. I filled him in on the finer arts of stealing: 1) make sure no one is looking and 2) always share the goodies with your superior – ME.

It took me some time to settle in to my new home – about four hours – that was dinner time. If I was going to be fed at this house, then I could begin to relax. I was allowed to sleep upstairs because there was no room for my 'four-poster' bed downstairs. I always go to bed at 9:30pm. It took them some time to understand this. I gave the message clear enough – one bark at the door – but they just weren't as bright as a guide dog and it had to be repeated several times every night for a few weeks before they got the message.

It seemed funny at first not to go to work, but we did go for a two-mile walk every morning. We passed a lake on the first day and I decided to go for a swim. I really enjoyed it, but they seemed to think I was going to die of heart failure – they don't know me; I'm going to live forever; I'm made of good stuff. We didn't go by the lake again. It was too worrying, they said. A pity really because I enjoy a good swim.

The most upsetting part of retiring was the unanimous family decision to put me on a diet. That's bad news for a Labrador, but there was little I could do about it. So, more walks, less food and I lost 5lbs. I must admit that I felt even fitter than when I retired – I could even play with Errol in the garden.

In March 1986 I was left with another puppy-walker for the day as my puppy-walker and family were going out. There was only room for one dog, so they took the baddie – Errol. I stayed with some very kind people; they left a 7lb turkey on the kitchen table for me. It went down well. (Well, I am retired.) They were a bit upset and worried in case I came to any harm (what… me??? I'm indestructible.) The carcass was thrown in the dustbin (spoilsports), but in the afternoon they let me into the garden, so I knocked the bin over and finished the carcass. This was a trick I had perfected when I was younger.

In April 1986 Errol went to Folly Court to be trained as a guide dog, and Lewis came to take his place. He was a good-looker, but I couldn't stand him – so I sulked. They know now that if I put my ears lower than my eyes I'm in a bad mood. We still went for our daily walks, but he would spoil them by charging into me – my back legs would give way and I would fall down. We went to the sea a couple of times. I enjoyed that; it was great to know I could still swim. Lewis didn't behave himself so he had to be tied up. I could then really enjoy myself with my ears up and a big smile on my face.

19th Feb 1987 – A great day for me. Lewis went to Folly Court. The next day we moved, only 300 yards away to a much bigger home, and my four-poster bed was put in the kitchen. I felt demoted, but it did mean that I didn't have to go upstairs. Just to keep in trim I went up every morning to see how the other half lived.

June 1987 – Blake came. He was a four-month-old Labrador. I liked him; he was fun but gentle. He went for a walk every morning but I declined some days, particularly if it was hot. The extra few hundred yards were a bit too much for me to cope with and my back legs were beginning to 'sag'. I still enjoyed a good walk in the park – I could do more sniffing than walking and we always went by car to get there.

January 1988 – Blake went and Ryan came. I missed Blake, but Ryan was gentle. He was three-quarters golden retriever. I didn't mind if he got into bed with me as long as he didn't fidget. I could even play with him – not as much as I did with

Blake because my back legs kept giving way, so I pretended to chase him and he did the running.

February 1988 – I was very ill, so ill that I refused food. I thought I was going to live forever, but I had my doubts then; I wasn't even sure if I'd get to my fourteenth birthday in March. The vet was kind. She gave me an injection and some antibiotic tablets and said to starve me for twenty-four hours and then, the best bit of all, a diet of chicken and rice. It took me about a month to recover, and I had to stop the occasional titbit as they upset me. I also had a bit of trouble with my anal gland – could be a tumour, they said.

Summer 1988 – I only managed a few short walks. I still went upstairs to see them each morning, but the stairs were getting steeper and I had to stop halfway to get my breath back. I fell downstairs once, but got up and walked away – after all, I'm Josie, and I could live forever.

October 1988 – Everything happened. I had another bad turn, more antibiotics, chicken and rice, and the good news – a long-lasting steroid injection. I'd recommend that to anyone in my condition. In a few days I was feeling a lot fitter. The vet said I was better than a lot of ten-year-olds. I got my appetite back, had a smile on my face and could cope with Ryan going and Lynton, a German Shepherd, coming. He shared my bed and I played with him – occasionally.

Josie shares her bed with Lynton

I don't go out for walks with him and I don't bother to go upstairs anymore – it isn't worth the effort – they all come down to me. In January 1989 I was having trouble getting into my four-poster bed, so they gave me a mattress on the floor. I'm beginning to feel my age these days, although I was fit enough to enjoy a party in March for my fifteenth birthday. Six of us, including Zelda (my successor), went to the park for a 'fun run' – I let the younger dogs do the running. I enjoyed wandering on the grass by the car. I can't do that often now – I'm beginning to feel my age. My front half is OK, but my back half is fading rapidly – my back legs are very weak and I'm worried about that tumour. I'm not doing much these days – just the occasional walk to the post office. Lynton is bigger than me and I'm afraid he's going to knock me over. I don't like going into the garden if he's there. I still enjoy my food – and the cat's food – but I spend most of my days sleeping on my bed.

May 1989 – Lynton caught kennel cough and then reacted to the antibiotics. For a few days I was livelier than him, but not any longer. It's June now and the days are hot and long, my back legs are very weak and that tumour is growing. I'm not enjoying my food and I find it difficult to get comfortable in my bed – the medication doesn't help anymore. I can't get better; she doesn't want to see me getting worse. I know what she's thinking – I can tell by the tears in her eyes. It's a difficult decision to make. We've had a good time together, but we both know it's time to call it a day. I don't want to live like this.

Josie – Guide Dog

Yellow Labrador Bitch

23rd March 1974 – 15th June 1989

Aged 15 years 3 months

R.I.P.

Lewis, the escapologist

B y now puppy-walking had become a way of life. It was not a question of whether I would have another puppy but when the next one would be coming and what it would be like. There was always great speculation around our dinner table about what puppies would be born, what their breed would be and most importantly what letter their name would begin with. The children were definitely hoping for a different letter of the alphabet each time, in the hopes of eventually walking the entire alphabet, whilst I was thinking that to walk twenty-five dogs (Guide Dogs don't use the letter X) seemed a little unrealistic – I would be nearly seventy by the time I finished if we did that.

Gus and Errol had both been pale-coloured Labradors. Secretly I preferred the darker golden-coloured dogs, so I was very pleased when my next dog Lewis, a Labrador crossed with a golden retriever, arrived because he was a very dark golden colour and very pretty, or should I say handsome. He was also very lively. He was even too lively for the retired guide dog Josie that we had at the time. He was the first new puppy she had encountered, and she sulked and returned to her rather grand, cushioned, four-legged bed, known as the four-poster bed, when he arrived.

Lewis, very handsome

In spite of his large amount of energy, Lewis's basic obedience was good, and he was the first puppy that I could get to 'sit' and 'lie down' when he was about ten feet away from me. I was very proud of this achievement and I could rely on him to do it first time, every time. Lewis did have other habits that unfortunately I could also rely on him doing whenever the opportunity arose. He loved rolling in unsavoury items, and there were many occasions on our return from a walk when he would need cleaning up before he could come into the house. I really don't like water and will do everything I can to prevent myself making a mess when I am doing a job. Messy jobs of any sort were definitely not good and cleaning a messy dog goes straight to the top of my least favourite occupations. Whenever I could, I delegated this one to Chris, but inevitably sometimes the job fell to me. In the end, we developed a good system of washing Lewis down using a bucket of soapy water and a sponge that were left permanently by the outside tap on the concrete patio; an old towel to dry him off was always hung near the outside tap, together with a pair of rubber gloves to use when the job fell to me. None of which added to the beauty of our patio area. One particular day, on a free run, Lewis managed to get himself covered, head, neck and shoulders, in very smelly matter. We were walking by the river at the time and there was a local lad playing hooky from school and fishing in the river just along the bank from us. This lad always spoke to me when I was out with the dogs. He was very good with them and all the dogs thought he was great. As usual, he called Lewis to him to stroke him. Knowing what a state Lewis was in, I started shouting as loudly as I could to warn the lad not to stroke Lewis because he had been rolling, but he didn't hear me. The wind was blowing in the wrong direction. Thankfully he had a very good sense of humour and beamed at me as he displayed his smelly hands. Perhaps that was his comeuppance for skiving off school.

Lewis's other special skill was opening doors. He would jump up, put his left paw on the handle, then his right one, and hey presto the door was open. He used these skills one night to gain access to our lounge, and when I came downstairs in the morning I found him totally relaxed and fast asleep on our settee. He had had a good night's sleep but this was certainly not a place that dogs were allowed. To solve this problem, we eventually put hook-and-eye catches on the top of all the doors to keep him out of the rooms he wasn't allowed in. Even then he managed to jump the stair gate and arrive upstairs in our bedroom. Not being at my best at night, I compromised, and he slept on the floor by my side of the bed – as good as gold I might add. There he stayed until the alarm went off in the morning and then, with one bounce, he was on the bed and full of himself. We were forever trying to be one step ahead of him and thinking outside the box for different ways to curb his exuberant and enthusiastic behaviour. Lewis kept us on our toes right up until he left us.

At about the time Lewis was due to go in for training, we were in the process of moving house and were gradually packing things from both the house and the garden. In a fairly stressed state one morning, while I was doing some washing, Lewis felt he needed to help me sort some of the items by taking them out of the washing basket, as I was trying to put them in the washing machine, and running off with them. This was the last thing I needed and so I put him in the garden out of my way. I had to lock the back door so that he didn't open it and let himself back in. He tried to open the door, jumping up at it a few times, and then he gave up and all went quiet. I was able to finish my job in peace. After about half an hour I opened the back door and called him, but he didn't come. This was strange, really, as a good recall was one of his specialities. I began to doubt that I had even put him in the garden and checked all the rooms in the house. No, he wasn't there, so I must have put him in the garden.

Then I decided that he must be at the end of the garden on the compost heap behind the shed – he had already been caught several times before snaffling things off it, and so I was fairly confident that this was where I would find him. I crept down the garden ready to catch him in the act, but he wasn't there either. Then my heart really started to pound. Where was he? Had I lost this valuable dog? I decided to phone the police to report him missing, but hoping that he had been found. I rang the police station and my call was quickly answered. "I'm ringing to report a missing dog."

"Can you describe it?"

I described him and the reply came back.

"Yes, we do have a dog of that description. He was found playing football with the cars on the A4."

I was so relieved when the police confirmed that a dog fitting his description had been found and was rather concerned that he had got as far as the very busy A4, about four roads away from our house. On the other hand, I was annoyed that no one had checked the discs on his collar and phoned either me or Guide Dogs to say he had been found.

David was at home ill at the time, so I had to get him out of bed to go and get Lewis from the police station, about three miles away, in Woodley. The policeman took me to the outside kennel at the back of the police station where Lewis had been put for safety. I identified Lewis in the kennel and was asked if he would run away if they let him out. Not a chance. Lewis was as relieved to see me as I was to see him. He was jumping and barking and was beside himself with joy. We went into the police station to do the paperwork, but it was difficult for me to hear the questions and for the policeman to hear my answers because Lewis was so vocal. When I got home with him, I went down the garden to see where he had escaped. That end of the garden was bordered by a hedge that had grown at least two feet higher than the dog-proof fencing and it seemed impossible that even Lewis could have jumped that. When I looked, we had moved a roll of chain-link fencing against the side fence and hedge in preparation for moving house. The only thing I could think was that he must have used that as a stepping stone to make his escape, although I still can't understand why he didn't choose to go to his favourite free run area when he knew the route to that so well.

A few days after this escapade, Lewis went to Wokingham to be trained as a guide dog. He spent about four months there and then moved with his trainer to another centre for his advanced training. He qualified, but was retired after a few months because of ill health. He had always been a healthy puppy but, after he had been working as a guide dog for a few months, he suffered from projectile vomiting caused by a blockage forming in the stomach. His problem was cured by an operation, but it was decided that it would be better if he was retired as a guide dog and re-homed as a pet.

When a dog is retired and the owner is unable to keep it, or if a puppy doesn't qualify as a guide dog, Guide Dogs commit to finding the dog a loving home for the rest of its life. Some puppies display traits that would make them suitable to become assistance dogs for 'Dogs for Good' or 'Hearing Dogs'. Others could be suitable as sniffer dogs or even a police dog and are offered to these organisations. If they are not suitable for any of these situations then the puppy is usually offered to the puppy-walker as a pet. The association also holds a list of people who have approached them about adopting a dog, have been interviewed by a member of Guide Dogs' staff and have been deemed suitable to own a dog. Some have requested a retired dog – usually an older dog but not always, as in the case of Lewis – while others would like a puppy. The dog would then be matched with people on this list whose home and situation would best suit the needs of the dog.

Lewis was still a young dog when he retired and I was asked if I would like him back as a pet. I was very tempted as I was quite fond of him and enjoyed working with him as his basic obedience was so good, but the family were less enthusiastic. I think they were enjoying not having Lewis arriving unexpectedly in their rooms, when they had forgotten to lock the door, and meeting them with so much exuberance, so reluctantly I said "No".

Teddy, our first cat

I t was while we were walking Lewis that we acquired our first cat. I had never owned a cat or been particularly fond of cats as pets, but a friend and neighbour, Barbara, who helped the local Cats Protection League, was asked to hand-rear four young kittens. They had been abandoned by their mother on a building site and were only a few days old at the time. Knowing we were animal lovers, she invited us to see them. They were tiny bundles of moving fur at the time and she kept them warm using blankets and hot water bottles. They needed feeding every three hours and so she was waking up in the night and giving them carefully measured amounts of warm milk delivered through a pipette.

That was a huge commitment and not something I could have done.

It's not often that you get the chance to handle such tiny kittens and they were a big hit with the whole family. In particular, Julie and David were very keen on them and made regular visits up the road to see the kittens and help feed them. Sadly, two of them died after ten days, but the other two survived – a female tabby, Millie, and a ginger tom, Teddy. When they were about five weeks old my friend went away on holiday so she asked Julie and David to look after them in our house. By this time the nighttime feeds had stopped, their eyes were open and they were eating solid kitten food, so this was manageable for the two of them and they did a brilliant job. Of course, they also became very fond of them and were very sad when they had to take the kittens back to Barbara when she came back from her holiday. In fact, they were so upset that Julie was reluctant to take them back and wanted to delegate the job to someone else. What they didn't know was that Barbara and I had agreed that they were going to be allowed to keep Teddy; Julie's friend was going to have Millie. I had to be really firm and make her take them back without letting the 'cat out of the bag' as I wanted them to hear from Barbara that they would be allowed to keep Teddy. Eventually they left, and reappeared five minutes later minus the cats. Barbara had asked if they would like to keep Teddy, but they hadn't thought they would be allowed to and had come back home to ask. They were delighted when I explained what had happened. They were asked to give a pound each donation to the Cats Protection League for their kitten, and very quickly raced back up the road with their pocket money clutched in their hands. So back to our house came Teddy, to become another member of our growing menagerie.

Teddy was quite happy living with the dogs, as he had lived with a dog since he was only a few days old. Sometimes I think he even thought he was a dog himself, as he shared so many of their habits. He enjoyed having a bone of his own when Josie and Lewis were given one, so when I went to the butcher's shop I would now bring back three dog bones instead of two. When the dogs were fed, Teddy was fed. He waited his turn with the others and was not bothered that he shared his eating space with a large Labrador puppy. I managed to train Lewis not to take Teddy's food, even though all food bowls were on the floor. When Lewis had eaten all his dinner he would sit about three feet away from Teddy's bowl and watch him eat all his dinner, drooling in anticipation. Teddy was a much slower eater than Lewis. To torment Lewis, Teddy would then sit about six inches away from his own empty bowl and spend a good five minutes cleaning himself. This task completed, he would stand up and casually walk away. This was the point at which I allowed Lewis to check out Teddy's bowl. There was never anything left in it, but Lewis always lived in hope.

Teddy and Lewis always got on really well. We had an open fire in our house which we lit regularly through the winter, and we have many photos of the two dogs and Teddy curled up on the floor in front of the fire with Teddy relaxed and leaning next to the larger dog's head. They even played together, and had a game which ended up with Teddy putting his head in Lewis's mouth. Lewis's retriever breeding came out then as he was so gentle with Teddy and no harm ever came to him.

Teddy was a playful kitten and interested in exploring everywhere he could. One day, around Christmas time, we had popped next door for Christmas drinks and left Julie, now fourteen, in charge at home. We had not been there long when the phone rang. It was Julie. "Mum, Teddy's gone up the chimney and I can't get him to come down. What should I do?" Thankfully there was no fire lit but I didn't have a wealth of cat experience to draw on, so I decided that what goes up must come down and that if she waited I was sure he would reappear. Sure enough, about five minutes later we had another call to say that he had reappeared, a little sooty but no worse off for his escapade.

When Teddy was about eight months old we moved house, only about a quarter of a mile away, but a larger house in a quieter road. Teddy made himself at home and soon discovered that he could get into the house through Julie's bedroom window. He climbed the forsythia hedge at the side of the house and, as we were now living in a chalet bungalow, he could walk along the tiles and climb through Julie's window, which was much easier than using a cat flap. He had become Julie's pet more than anyone else's and would spend the night curled up asleep on her bed. I don't like animals on the beds, but soon discovered that it was very difficult to stop a cat, especially when he was aided by my daughter. He would come when she called him, and from a young kitten would climb up and sit on her shoulders whilst she walked around the house. This looked very cute when he was a small cat, but was more unwieldy as he grew older and required very good balance.

Teddy's life was a short but merry one. He was only eighteen months old when he was seriously injured by a car just outside our house. At 11.15pm there was a knock at the door and a man, holding an injured cat, asked if we knew who it belonged to. He hadn't bumped into him but saw him lying in the road. It was, of course, Teddy.

We brought him indoors, wrapped him in some of his bedding, put him in a cardboard box and phoned the vet. Within five minutes we were on an eight-mile car journey to the vet. I have always said that I don't want a three-legged animal but when, at 11.30pm, a very distraught daughter said, "If he needs to have his leg amputated, Mum, can we have it done?" all my principles went out of the window and my answer was "Yes". The journey took ages, especially as no one wanted to talk. We took Teddy into the surgery, where the vet opened the box to examine him. He did not need to have a leg amputated as he had not survived the serious internal injuries. It was a sad journey home and quite a few tears were shed that night by both young and old.

New house and new pups, Blake and Ryan

L ewis was not the sort of dog you need helping when you are moving house, and so it was quite a relief that he had reached the right age and maturity to leave us just before we moved. In fact, Lewis left us the day before we moved house, and so on our moving day we had just Josie.

We weren't moving far, just down the road, but to a detached chalet bungalow with bigger bedrooms and more living space downstairs. In particular, we wanted a bigger bedroom for David as up until now he had had the little box room which had barely enough room for a bed and small chest of drawers in it. All the children had been round the new house and each had chosen their new bedroom. Julie wasn't keen on the change of house and was threatening a sit in, Mark wouldn't have minded either way, but David was really excited about moving to a new house. We were really pleased about this, although it turned out that it was not because he would have a bigger room but because there was a large fish pond in the garden with several fish in it. This shouldn't have surprised us as David was a big animal lover already.

We moved house on my birthday and celebrated both new house and birthday in style with a fish and chip supper sitting around our newly moved-in dining room table. I think we had definitely earned it that day. Most of our household goods had gone in the removal van, but some things didn't travel well that way. It must have been quite a sight to see the children traipsing down the road carefully carrying a bowlful of goldfish, followed not long after by a hamster cage complete with hamster.

I found the new house very quiet, but it wasn't until the buses were temporarily re-routed down our road that I realised that that was the sound I had been missing. I began to feel at home in our new house, and after a few months I was getting dog withdrawal symptoms and asked for another pup. Our new home had the luxury of a good-sized utility room on the side of the kitchen, which had a stable door opening onto a covered area in front of the garage, with a side gate onto the garden and double doors at the front opening onto the drive. This time I got a four-month-old yellow Labrador called Blake. He needed to be re-homed and so I agreed to take him on. He came with the reputation of being a quiet pup, but I had my doubts. Within seconds of coming into our house, he was rushing around madly and behaving like an over-excited young pup. Even with all my new doggy facilities, this behaviour was going to be very difficult to handle, and I was beginning to wonder what I had agreed to have.

After a couple of days Blake calmed down and was in fact a very gentle dog. I think he was unable to cope with all the change and had reacted in a hyperactive way. Despite all the indications given by his lively start, Blake's stay with us was very uneventful. He turned out to be a calm and placid dog who responded well to all the training. He got on with the household menagerie, never once challenged Josie for her role as 'top dog' and managed not to upset any of the family or our friends. He had no major health problems and was easy to exercise and groom. I sent a model dog into kennels for further training.

Blake found the move to the Guide Dog kennels at the end of his time with us very challenging. My theory about his original hyperactive behaviour being set off by changes that he couldn't cope with was backed up when he left us, as this behaviour showed itself again when he was in kennels. As puppy-walkers, we are given reports on our dogs by the different trainers that work within the organisation. Sometimes it is a written report – much like a school report – and other times it can be a phone call. I keep all my dogs' reports with as much pride as my children's. They are to me testament to the work I do. In a phone call, Blake's trainer described his behaviour in kennels as very wild. I told him of my experience with Blake when he had first arrived with us and said that I felt that it would improve when he was taken out of the kennel environment. This proved to be so, and when Blake qualified he was placed with a very quiet, kind man, a perfect match for both dog and owner.

It is unusual to have an overlap of puppies – the old one still being with you when the new one arrives – but it does sometimes occur when the older puppy is doing well and there are lots of new puppies needing homing. This is what happened with Blake when Ryan came, and showed how Blake had grown into a sensible adult dog – ideal to make a guide dog.

Ryan was my puppy for Christmas as he arrived between Christmas Day and New Year's Day, but a guide dog pup is for a year, not just for Christmas. He was affectionately known as 'Ryan the Lion' because he had a habit of making a very vocal throaty noise when he was happy, was a lovely golden colour and very cuddly. He was three-quarters golden retriever and one-quarter Labrador. His father was a golden retriever and his mother was a Labrador/golden retriever cross. At an early age, he showed himself to be a much more confident and pushy dog than Blake ever was.

Ryan walked well from an early age and nothing fazed him – well, not a lot, anyway. Sounds didn't bother him, but he sometimes took issue with things that he saw. I think this must have been the retriever in him, and he certainly responded with typical retriever stubbornness. His first problem was with orange traffic cones. I don't know if it was their shape or colour, but he certainly couldn't possibly pass them. So he just stood and looked. I tried using some of the tricks of the trade to get him past them, such as going up to the cones and touching them myself or offering him very tasty treats. The only successful method was patience. I just had to stand and wait for him to decide that they weren't a problem and then he walked past as if nothing had happened. This could take at least three minutes – a long time when standing on the corner of a very busy junction. He had the same reaction to workmen in orange jackets. I think he must have been long-sighted as he could spot trouble a long way off.

The local garden centre also posed a problem

one day. I was walking to the main entrance with Ryan beside me when, all of a sudden, the lead went taught. I had continued walking in whilst Ryan had spotted a problem and was stationary behind me. Now what was his issue? No road cones to be seen anywhere, not even a long way away, and no workmen in orange jackets either. This time it was two ornamental lions, about five feet high, either side of the entrance. I hadn't even noticed they were there, but there was no way he could possibly walk past them. Perhaps seeing two of his namesakes was more than he could cope with. I tried all my usual tricks, but all to no avail. He had dug his retriever heels in and that was that. We were going nowhere. I had to once again apply my patience and wait.

At least five minutes later Ryan showed no sign of relenting and, desperate to go to the garden centre, I gave in and went in through a side entrance; it was probably an exit, really. I did my shopping and came out, without thinking, through the main entrance past the lions. No problem for Ryan this time. Just to test the system I turned around and went back into the shop past the lions. Ryan followed and took no notice that time or any other time that we visited the garden centre during his stay with us. To this day I have no idea what made him take a dislike to them and why they were suddenly no problem at all.

As Ryan grew older he grew into a mini excavator. Digging holes in the garden was his speciality. He

Ryan the mini excavator

could get head, shoulders and chest into the ground in no time at all and apparently with very little effort. He was confident enough to make the most of any opportunity to have a quick dig when he thought we weren't looking, but when caught in the act he'd stop immediately but show no signs of remorse.

He turned out to be less confident on bonfire night when we had a few fireworks in the back garden. My parents came to join us, but my mother stayed in the lounge with their dog, Lyn, a cairn terrier, and Ryan, with the television on to mask the sound of the bangs. My mother was elderly and suffered from asthma. This way she could sit on the sofa in the lounge looking through the patio doors down the garden, enjoying the fireworks without having to worry about the cold or the sounds, and we would not have to worry about the dogs.

Our mini display of rockets and Roman candles went well, and when the fireworks had finished I went inside to check that the dogs were all right. I should have gone earlier. Ryan had been frightened by the noise and decided to get on the sofa with my mother for comfort. As I walked through the door I could see Ryan leaning heavily against my mother who, although a dog lover, was quite a frail lady weighing about seven stone, and having a very large dog leaning into her was not such a comfort for her as it was for the dog. Unfortunately, she had not been able to get him down from the sofa and was very grateful that I had arrived. Ryan was very obedient and with a quick command 'Off!' he was soon back on the lounge floor where he should have been and my mother was feeling a lot more comfortable.

Ryan eventually left us and qualified as a guide dog quite quickly. He had just the right balance of pushiness and obedience that made him able to make decisions in the best interests of his owner. His owner contacted me once Ryan qualified and I learned that he still had issues with road cones, but he had learned to live with a guide dog that had that quirk.

Miffy, the feral kitten

It was about four months after Teddy died that we got another cat. We decided to get another rescue cat, but this time it was to be one with a different upbringing. We contacted the Cats Protection League which had rescued a litter of kittens nearby that we could go and visit to see if we would like to choose one of them. The kittens had been discovered in a garden under a bush where they had been reared by their feral mother before being rescued at about six weeks old. They were being kept in a lady's house in Maidenhead. There were cats everywhere, in the hall, kitchen and lounge. We didn't see in the bedrooms but I wouldn't have been at all surprised if they were in there as well. They were sitting or lying on the floor, chairs and tables, and were even on the top of the kitchen work surfaces and the tops of the kitchen wall cupboards. There must have been at least thirty cats, all of which had been rescued for some reason or other. I had never seen so many cats in one place before. It was quite eerie. If the house had been full of dogs they would have rushed up to greet us, but the cats just sat and watched. Some things make an impression that lasts a lifetime, and this was one of them.

The kittens that we had come to see were in the bathroom, where we were taken to see them. In particular, Julie was taken by a small pale tabby, one with grey, pink and white fur. When Julie picked her up she clung very tightly to her and didn't move. We felt this was an omen that she was the cat for us and took her home. We were soon to realise that this behaviour wasn't the sign of an affectionate animal, but that of one which was scared stiff.

Julie decided to call her Miffy, a name that she had taken from her childhood books about Miffy, a white rabbit. Teddy had been hand-reared from a few days old and was a very tame cat. Miffy, on the other hand, was a true feral cat and had lived life in the wild until she had been rescued at about six weeks old. Her behaviours had been learned from her first six weeks when she had learned to be wary of people, and her introduction to our household must have been very frightening for her.

We came home with our new pet and made her comfortable in the utility room. We left her there on her own so that she could settle into her new home without too much fussing from us, as we knew she was feral and a lot less used to humans than Teddy had been. After we had eaten our dinner we went to see how she was. 'How she was' wasn't the right question; 'Where was she?' was what we wanted to know. Although only a small room, our new cat was nowhere to be seen. We came to the conclusion that she must be hiding. There were only three places she could be: behind, or even in, the boiler, behind the washing machine, or in, or behind, the sink cupboard unit. We pulled out the washing machine: no luck there. We looked in the cupboard and took the back off, but she wasn't there. The boiler was the only place left. Off came the casing of the boiler, but she wasn't there either. We knew she was a very small kitten, but surely she couldn't fit into thin air?

There was one last glimmer of hope. We had left the top window of the utility room open on the first notch to ventilate the room. There was a gap of about one inch, so perhaps she had gone through that. In desperation we continued our search outside in the adjacent garage. Eventually we found her there on a shelf about six feet off the ground. I still find it difficult to comprehend that Miffy, as such a tiny kitten, could have got from the floor onto the work surface, then up to the top window, out through such a small gap and finish up on a high shelf in the garage. It was probably these skills that had made her a survivor as a feral kitten.

When Miffy joined our family, Ryan, our puppy at that time, was about eight months old. Miffy wasn't very worried about Ryan, and Ryan ignored Miffy. It wasn't long before Miffy, although still unwilling to show herself to strangers, was perfectly happy in our house and had settled well into the family. She slept in Julie's bedroom and used an open upstairs window which gave her free access in and out of the house to the garden. She was fed on the work surface in the utility room out of the way of the dogs. It was a few months after her arrival that Miffy was to meet her first six-week-old puppy. This was Lynton, a German Shepherd dog.

My puppy-walking supervisor arrived. She left Lynton in the car whilst we did the paperwork, and Miffy, with a stranger in the house, kept a low profile. Once the paperwork was complete our little puppy was brought in. We all made a fuss of him and the supervisor left us to enjoy him. I decided that he might need to 'busy' and so let him out into the garden to see if he would do anything. This was when Miffy made her appearance. Even at this age Lynton was a few pounds heavier than she was but, undeterred by this, she went in for the attack. Facing him, she put out her right front leg, and pulled his left front leg under his body. He fell down and within seconds she had Lynton on his back and stood over him pinning him to the ground. I rushed out to rescue my puppy, with visions of Lynton being bitten or his eyes being scratched by her and me being banned from puppy-walking all the time we had this aggressive cat.

My supervisor phoned the next day to see how Lynton was settling in. It was with trepidation that I explained to her how Miffy was attacking him. To my relief, she wasn't worried about my cat attacking her dog, but much more concerned that Lynton wasn't hurting Miffy. For the first week Miffy won these battles every time, leaving a rather shocked little puppy in her wake. After a few weeks Lynton had grown, the roles were completely reversed and Miffy was being bowled over by him. At this stage they called a truce and, with healthy mutual respect in place, Miffy gave in gracefully. When he was full grown I even saw Lynton at times with his mouth wide open and Miffy sitting in front of him with her head in his mouth. It was all fun and games and they remained best of friends for the rest of their lives.

Miffy was a hunter and occasionally brought her prey home. Waking up to half a dead goldfish on the bedroom floor was not the best way to start the day. Another time I went into Julie's bedroom and found the remains of a dead pigeon, mainly feathers, all over the room. Julie was at college at the time but due home for the holidays the next day, so I decided to leave the mess for her to clear up on her arrival – after all, Miffy was her cat. I rang her at college… "Your cat has caught a pigeon. It's your cat and it's in your room. I've decided to leave it for you to sort out when you get home."

Julie arrived back from Plymouth the next day all ready for the big clear up, which was a good job as she couldn't actually unpack or get into her room until she had done the job, as there were so many feathers everywhere.

Julie set about the task in good spirits and, as she vacuumed up the last few feathers, she heard a rattling sound in the vacuum cleaner. After further investigation she discovered that it was a small white ring, just the right size for a bird's leg, with a telephone number written on it. The pigeon must have been a homing pigeon. There was nothing for it – she needed to telephone the number and explain what had happened to the bird. Julie carefully dialled the number and tactfully explained that she had found the dead bird, not mentioning that her cat had killed it. The owners were quite philosophical about it, saying they had recently moved to the area, that this was a problem they were having, and they offered to come and collect the bird. They were very thankful when Julie explained that she had in fact already dealt with it – she didn't mention that it was in her room and she couldn't go to bed until she had removed the evidence. Then they explained that they had been having lots of trouble with cats, to which Julie kept very quiet and just made sympathetic noises in agreement, quickly finishing the conversation. It turned out that their house was only one hundred yards away from us as the crow flies, or in this case as the pigeon flies. Mark commented that it was a pretty useless bird to get lost such a short distance from home.

One thing I have always enjoyed about our pets is seeing how they respond to each other and seeing their individual characters come out. Miffy soon developed her own collection of idiosyncrasies. She had practised her fishing skills inside before transferring them to fishing in the garden pond. She used to sit on the kitchen windowsill, carefully watching the two goldfish in the tank, which was also on the windowsill, but never succeeded in catching one. We put a cake rack weighted down with a stone to make a cover over the top of the tank to keep the fish safe, but there was a small gap, just wide enough for Miffy's paw, at one end of the tank. Miffy would stand at the end of the tank squinting through the gap to work out where the fish were. She would then move her face and put her paw through the gap to reach the place where she had last seen the fish. Needless to say, she never managed to catch them as they had always moved by the time she put her paw in the gap, but this activity kept her entertained for hours.

Miffy fishing

Later, Miffy progressed to the garden pond. It was a dull, grey Saturday afternoon when she was sitting on the edge of the pond watching the large fish with a view to catching one. She crouched and went to dip her paw in the water after the fish, but the water was lower from the edge of the pond than she had realised – she lost her balance and fell in with a splash. Everyone within hearing distance looked up just in time to see Miffy as she climbed out, shook herself and sat on the edge of the pond looking like the proverbial drowned rat – but trying to restore her dignity by pretending it hadn't happened.

Miffy always was a timid cat and ran upstairs whenever the front doorbell rang. It was some time before my puppy-walking supervisor even saw our cat. Her reaction was different when Julie came home. Often Miffy would sit on the ridge of the roof of the house, silhouetted against the sky, waiting for her. When Julie arrived she would call to Miffy as she walked down the drive. By the time Julie had opened the front door, Miffy would have come down from the roof, in through the open bedroom window and raced down the stairs just in time to meet her as she walked in through the door. She would then do an impression of a parrot by sitting on Julie's shoulder as she walked around the house.

Miffy had far more road sense than Teddy and was with us for much longer. We were grateful not to have to deal with another incident of a cat that had been run over by a car, and she saw several puppies come and go. She had learnt her lesson with Lynton, though, and after a half-hearted attempt to bowl over the next puppy she gave up playing with the puppies and just looked over them with a watchful eye from afar.

10

Lynton, the German Shepherd dog

"Why not have a German Shepherd next time?" asked my supervisor. "I'd love to; however, my mother-in-law is afraid of them. If you get desperate, give me a ring and I'll see how she feels about it," I replied. I should have realised that German Shepherd dogs are only usually placed with experienced puppy-walkers and the puppy would have been more difficult to place than a Labrador.

Three days later… "I'm really desperate. I have a German Shepherd dog who is prospective breeding stock. None of the other centres can find anyone to walk him and if you can't have him he'll probably have a career change."

I put the situation to my mother-in-law, who said that if I wanted him I should have him. Every time my supervisor had asked what I wanted to walk next, I'd said, "I'd like something different." I was keen to try the challenge of walking a German Shepherd, but never thought I would be able to because of my mother-in-law's fear. This would probably be my one and only opportunity. I said I would keep him out of her way when she visited and all would be fine. Then I rang my supervisor to accept the puppy.

So, my Shepherd came. He arrived late in the day. He seemed very frail – only weighing seven pounds, his eyes were quite red and his travelling companion had been sick all over him. I have to confess I was a bit disappointed when I saw him. He was called Lynton. Several people commented that Linton was a sickly man in the book *Wuthering Heights*, so I even read the book to check the facts – no mean feat for a non-book reader like myself. As his name was spelt with a 'Y' and not an 'I', I could only relate his name to the disaster towns of Lynton and Lynmouth. Either way, we were backing a loser as far as his name was concerned.

Josie, our resident fourteen-year-old retired guide dog, took him under her wing and let him sleep in her bed under the kitchen table – and even shared it with him, as long as he didn't move. Previous pups had not been so privileged. Maybe there was something good going for this young puppy, as Josie seemed to approve of him.

Lynton had a few digestive problems. We very quickly worked out he couldn't digest biscuits or rice, and for a few weeks he ate only chicken. After trying a variety of foods we eventually discovered that a diet of meat and wholemeal bread didn't upset his stomach, and he lived on this. He was healthy, but was always rather bony. At least, being long-haired, he didn't look so thin.

This was the first Shepherd that I had walked, and I soon discovered that the general public's attitude to a Shepherd is different to that of a Labrador or a golden retriever. When his ears were

Lynton as a pup

floppy, people would say, "Oh, isn't he lovely – but he'll be vicious when he grows up." "No, he won't," I'd say. "He's going to be a guide dog." I had a feeling at this stage that I was the aggressive one. The problem disappeared when his ears went up. Nobody spoke to me at all then. At least I could take him out for a walk without any interruptions.

German Shepherd dogs have a tendency to be 'one-man dogs', so part of walking Lynton was to make sure he was friendly with everyone, including the family, all our friends and the general public. He was an intelligent, very trainable and highly sensitive dog. His sensitivity was highlighted when Julie's friend Louise came round one day. Louise grew up in a dog-free household, but was used to our dogs and had learnt to cope with her friend living in a house full them. On the afternoon in question, Louise arrived on her bike and brought it in through the side gate and into the covered passageway at the side of the house. Lynton heard the sound of footsteps and the bike being pushed through the gravel as it approached the door. He started barking at the sound to ward off the intruder. Louise continued with what she was doing and walked in through the side gate with her bike, all ready to put it in the garage. When she saw Lynton still barking she looked at him, saying, "Don't be so silly, Lynton!" and then continued moving her bike. This completely threw him. He stopped barking, his tail went between his legs and he ran back out into the garden. Louise put her bike away and then sat in the kitchen chatting with Julie and me. Lynton then decided he wanted to come in, but he had to get past the 'intruder' first. He slunk into the kitchen and, giving Louise as wide a berth as possible, moved around the edge of the kitchen with his back to the cupboards until he had got past her and could escape into the rest of the house. From this response, I don't think he would have made a very good guard dog.

There were several situations where Lynton was suspicious, such as meeting tall men with beards or men wearing hats and gloves. At the time there was a police station in Twyford and I would often see policemen in uniform walking in the village. Lynton would look at them warily, so I took the opportunity to ask if I could stop and talk with them for a few minutes so that my dog could get used to them. Well, it was a bit different to asking them the time.

To really help Lynton conquer his fear of men in hats and gloves, Mark's friend helped us out. He loved Lynton and the feeling was mutual. When he was coming to visit we arranged for various different items of clothing to be left outside for him to put on before he came into the house. The first couple of times Lynton was suspicious, but very quickly realised that people wearing hats, gloves and dark coats could even be one of your favourite people and there was nothing to be afraid of.

Guide dog puppies have to be able to travel in cars and on public transport. He was happy riding in my car and on buses, but trains were different. It wasn't so much the travelling on trains, but getting on and off them. The main Reading to Paddington line goes through Twyford. There is also a branch line from Twyford to Henley. This train will wait for five to ten minutes for passengers transferring from the mainline trains to the Henley train. This was a convenient place to practise getting on and off a train.

On my first attempt I managed to coax him onto the train using titbits and friendly persuasion. He walked up and down the length of the carriage; I sat on a seat and he lay on the floor next to me. Then we got up to get off together. This is where the system broke down. His fear of getting off was worse than the fear of getting on. I think it was the combination of the wide gap between the platform and the carriage and the sound of the engine vibrating underneath him. He was not coming off. He dug his heels in and pulled away from the door. Neither coaxing nor pulling him worked. He was not going to move. I had visions of going to Henley and back on the train all day, until I was rescued by the station master. I explained my problem and he kindly got on board the train, took off one of the seats and made a ramp from the train to the platform: 'Problem solved,' said Lynton and walked off the train as if he was royalty. I couldn't practise any more that day as the train was waiting to depart, but the following day I went back to the station and Lynton got on and off the train without any hesitation.

Lynton was a highly intelligent dog and quickly learned all that a puppy needs to know, but his health needed careful management all the time he was with us. At eight months old he caught kennel cough. When dogs get kennel cough they develop a rasping cough that continues for a while and is highly contagious. If you have more than one dog it is likely that they will all catch it. In this case it led to complications which had to be treated with antibiotics. Lynton was given an antibiotic but was allergic to it. He was continually sick, had diarrhoea and didn't move. We had three visits to the vet in one day, but for the next twenty-four hours he was really ill and there was nothing we or the vet could do but wait and see what happened. It was about twenty-four hours before he started showing signs of recovery and got to his feet to wander around. He was on the mend. Fortunately, Lynton recovered, but I had definitely gained a few grey hairs from the episode.

Lynton was nine months old when Josie died. He had been very attached to Josie, and he was the only dog that Josie had allowed to share her basket under the island bench in the centre of the kitchen.

I thought that Lynton would rush at the chance to sleep under the kitchen table with plenty of space and the basket to himself but, from the day she died, he never slept under there again. He really was a very sensitive dog.

For the next five months Lynton became my special friend. We went everywhere together and I no longer felt I was puppy-walking. He was so mature. We had conquered his earlier fear of trains – well, the gap between the platform and the train – and tall men with beards, hats, dark coats and gloves were no longer the problem they had been. Walking my dog was a pleasure and no longer a job.

Julie was at college in Plymouth at this time and occasionally she came home for the weekend. We would meet her at Reading station, so it was a good opportunity to take Lynton with us to get as much experience of trains and stations as possible. Being a Friday evening, it was particularly busy. We had to wait about fifteen minutes for the train from Plymouth to arrive. Lynton waited patiently on the platform and ignored all the activity that was around him. Eventually, Julie's train arrived. She got off and walked along the platform towards us. When she was about fifteen yards away from us, Lynton spotted her in the crowd. He was beside himself with excitement and began to howl at the top of his voice, which could be heard easily above the general hustle and bustle in the station. He even forgot himself and jumped up at Julie, putting his paws on her shoulders. Heads turned, wondering what was happening. We were feeling very embarrassed, but Julie was thrilled to receive such a welcome.

Soon after this the time came for Lynton to leave us to be trained as a guide dog. By now he had completely won my mother-in-law's affection. He would always sit by her feet when she visited us, and she would stroke him saying that she still didn't like Shepherds – but Lynton was different. And he was a complete favourite with the whole family. He was now eating meat and biscuit, and weighed seventy pounds. Still a bit bony but, being a long-haired dog, he looked fine – in fact, he was a good-looking dog. I sent him off with my usual: "Work hard, find a good owner, but if you don't qualify as a guide dog you can come back." Some hopes – our best dog out of seven pups. Since the first six had made it, there was no way that Lynton would not qualify.

I saw his trainer occasionally at puppy classes. "How's he getting on?" I'd ask. "Fine," she'd say, but did admit once that he had a digestive problem. She didn't say that he was losing weight and had gone down to sixty pounds at one stage. A good job, as I would have been really worried. After four months, Lynton went onto advanced training and was due to take part in the demonstration on Supporters' Day at Folly Court, the Wokingham Training Centre, four weeks later. A week before

Supporters' Day I had a telephone call from Alan Brooks, the dog training manager. "I'm afraid I have some bad news for you about Lynton." My heart sank and I thought that he must have died. He continued by saying that Lynton had a pancreatic deficiency and, although there were several working dogs with this problem, Lynton's was complicated and they had decided to give him a career change. I can't remember what he said after that – I was just waiting for a break in the conversation so that I could say, "Can I have him back?" I didn't care at that stage how ill he was – I was just relieved to hear that he was still alive.

Within two hours, my son David and I were at Folly Court to collect him. He was definitely thin but I had forgotten how tall he was. When he recognised us he was so happy and excited to see us that he couldn't contain himself. He began to howl, jumped up at David and pushed him into the newly planted privet hedge around the 'toileting pen'. I'm glad to say the hedge suffered no long-term effects. We came home to the rest of the family with one excited dog, a sack of special dog food, some medication and a list of instructions: "Three meals a day, one tablet half an hour before a feed, eight tablets after each meal. Twenty-seven tablets a day." As I opened his jaw to put in the first tablet, I was quite relieved he wasn't aggressive.

After a couple of years, I learned to live with

Lynton's digestive problems – my friends may tell you otherwise – and, for such a sick dog, we had only two or three visits to the vet during the next five years. One of these visits was after a walk with my friend and her dog Bonnie, Lynton and my latest puppy Hobo. We were walking down an unmade-up road that leads to the River Thames. There are houses on one side of the top half of the road but at the bottom half there is a ditch on either side, and then fields fenced with barbed wire. In this section, the dogs can be free running, and on a hot day a dip in the ditch adds to their enjoyment. At one point I called Hobo, who came back to me with blood on his head. I checked him for cuts, but realised the blood was superficial and must have dripped on him from one of the other dogs. It turned out that Lynton was the injured dog. On close examination I could see that he had torn his ear on some of the barbed wire and it was split down about two inches from the tip. It was about 2.30pm by this time, but as the vets' surgery wasn't open until 4pm we finished our walk then went home and I booked an appointment. I must have had a mental block as I remembered later that vets are available for emergencies anytime night or day. What a heartless dog owner I was. Always a good patient, Lynton allowed the vet to check his ear without complaint. The vet was surprised at the length of the tear – it needed at least five stitches to repair it.

Back home as a pet, there were free runs on the agenda every day. There was now no need to take him on buses and trains. It seemed strange to go to the local shop at the end of the road and have to tie my dog to the ring provided outside the shop. Now he was a 'pet' and not a 'guide dog puppy in training' I could not take him in with me. On a free run, Lynton did have a tendency to make sure any other dogs with us, including the pup in training, behaved themselves. Lynton's recall was good, and if I called the puppy's name at the same time and it didn't respond immediately Lynton would wait about five yards away from me and have a word in its ear before it got to me. This created an interesting situation. The puppy didn't want to come to me because it had to pass Lynton on the way, but the longer it delayed the longer it was reprimanded by Lynton. After a few months I solved the problem by first calling the pup, or any other dogs that were with me. When they reached me I then called Lynton.

Lynton liked to carry a stick in his mouth whenever he went on a walk. We kept a mini log pile of suitable pieces of wood by the back door – ones that were about eighteen inches long with a diameter of about one and a half inches. At the beginning of the walk we selected one for him to take and he would carry it until he reached a free run area and then we were expected to throw it for him to retrieve. He always brought the same stick back to us. There was an added benefit to Lynton carrying a stick. It preoccupied him and he ignored any other dogs, allowing them to relax and enjoy the walk without being a part of Lynton's dog training regime, which didn't always match mine.

Most of our local walks are in meadows with only a few pieces of stick around. Once a week I met up with puppy-walking friends who lived five miles away. They always walked their dogs in wooded areas. Lynton took his stick with him and as usual we threw it for him to retrieve. I was always impressed that he managed to find his stick among all the pieces of wood on the ground. Well, he nearly always found it. There were a few occasions when he couldn't track it down. When this happened we tried to interest him in an alternative stick – plenty to choose from in a wood – but none of them could replace the lost one. When he had lost his stick, he was cross. He seemed to think all the other dogs were to blame and went back to discipline them for the rest of the walk.

Occasionally, Lynton's dog training skills did come in handy. On one of these times I was travelling with a puppy-walking friend in her car to go for a walk with our dogs. We had four dogs with us: her pet dog Tudor, Lynton and our respective ten-month-old guide dog pups. The young dogs were excited to see each other and were generally playing around in the back of the car and being a nuisance.

We tried using our best authoritative verbal control with words such as 'Quiet!' and 'Enough!', without any success at all. After a couple of minutes Lynton must have felt sorry for us, or had just had enough of the unruly dogs himself. Sitting bolt upright in the back of the car he gave one short, commanding bark. That did the trick – instant silence. We even stopped talking as we couldn't bring ourselves to disturb the peace. How I wish I had had that bark recorded. There have been several situations since where it would have come in very useful.

A few years later Lynton's health problems began to get the better of him and were no longer easy to manage. He began to vomit bile occasionally in the mornings and ate less and less. Since he was a German Shepherd and not food-driven like Labradors, I didn't worry too much, until the day came that he ate nothing and refused to go for a walk. He must have been feeling very ill to refuse a walk.

We went to see the vet. By now, Lynton weighed sixty-five pounds. He was diagnosed as having chronic kidney failure, anaemia and loss of muscle mass. No cure – we could only try and stabilise the problem. He was put on a low fat diet and monthly steroid injections. The improvement was instant. His appetite was better than it had ever been, but the pancreatic problem couldn't cope with the low protein diet. So a compromise was made and medium-protein food was on the menu.

This treatment, plus antibiotics for a high bacteria count, worked wonders. He put on weight and reached seventy-five pounds. There was a temporary setback when he tore a toenail. He couldn't have it removed because of the dangers of an anaesthetic to a dog with kidney failure. It took him a couple of months to get better but by then he was beginning to drag his hind legs and his toenails were wearing away – signs of the start of nerve degeneration.

By the end of 1995 he was heading down the slippery slope. He drank more, ate less, lost weight and dragged his hind legs more – but still looked fit and well and always wanted a walk. The bottom of the slope was reached on 11th March. He was seven and a half years old and it was exactly eleven months after the kidney failure had been diagnosed.

I phoned the vet in the morning to arrange for him to come to my house and put Lynton to sleep. He couldn't come until after all the morning consultations, which would be about 1pm. It was a long time to wait having made the decision – nearly five hours. I needed to keep my mind occupied, so as it was a guide dog puppy training class that day I decided to take my latest puppy Rudge there. I felt it would be better than sitting at home crying, which might also have upset Lynton. I didn't tell anyone at puppy class about Lynton in case I burst into tears. On reflection it was probably the best place to have had a good cry surrounded by about a dozen dog lovers.

Once back home I sat with Lynton for about half an hour before the vet came. In my experience vets are excellent in this situation. You can trust that they will not put an animal down unless it is the right thing to do, but are also very aware of how you feel as a pet owner. When you are emotionally attached to an animal, what might seem like the obvious decision to everyone else is not an obvious or easy decision for you. When the vet came Lynton was lying in his bed at the side of the utility room, and we both went and joined him. The vet carefully looked Lynton over and assessed his health, reassuring me that I had made the right decision. He let me say my final goodbyes before giving Lynton the injection, and we both watched as he slipped peacefully away. Having made the decision I knew it was the right one and I actually felt better for having made it.

We were lucky to have had our favourite dog back home – and although he was ill, he never looked like a sick dog. He was always lively, willing to go anywhere and everywhere. A lot of the credit must go to the vet for his medical expertise, to the Guide Dogs' kennel staff for giving me a shoulder to cry on – even if it was at the end of the phone – and last but by no means least, the drug companies who produced in the region of 58,400 tablets which Lynton had taken in the six years after being back with us. At least 1,000 of them were antibiotics, which he had in his last ten months. I've checked the maths and I keep coming up with the same answer.

He will always be special. He was great with the pups – especially during their 'teenage years'. I am now realising that one bark from Lynton had far more effect than ten words from me. We have a framed photo of him up on the kitchen wall. It is taken from the 1991 Guide Dogs calendar, where Lynton appeared in the July/August page. The writing underneath says: 'Lynton, a long-haired German Shepherd dog. The association covers the cost of food and pays veterinary bills. A comprehensive after-care and support service is provided for all Guide Dog Owners.' In Lynton's case, this was extended to a career-change dog and his puppy-walker – and received with many thanks.

G.S.D. – OK

You've walked them now for many years,
Those Labradors with floppy ears,
The moulting coat, the thrashing tails,
The digging paws, the wimpish wails,
Those saucer eyes and little brain
(They've got it wrong – they *like* the rain!).
You've many pictures, memories too
About the evil things they do.
Well, now it's changed and you can talk
About the proper dog to walk.
This Christmas gift will help create
A book to set the record straight.
The noble head, the honest stare,
The sculptured pose – I'm nearly there.
Afraid of naught, well, almost right,
Don't like trains and cars at night,
Tall, dark strangers, omnibus
And all those folks who make a fuss.
You must admit, a G.S.D.
Is just the thing, your cup of tea.
So why the blazes cock it up
And get another yellow pup?

By Chris Easton
(The gift was a photo album)

11

Varley; they can't all make it as a guide dog

By this time puppy-walking had become a way of life, and it wasn't long after Lynton went into training that we were ready to receive our next pup. This time we were back to the more usual breed of dog used by Guide Dogs – the Labrador. They are generally intelligent, sociable, relatively easy to train and can cope with almost anything life throws at them.

The association runs its own breeding programme of puppies from their centre in Warwickshire. Stud dogs and brood bitches are chosen for the suitable characteristics they demonstrate, and as a breeding animal reaches retirement age staff look to replace them with a dog or bitch that shows the same traits that make a good guide dog. Often they will identify pups in the animal's later litters as potential breeding stock and select a replacement from that line. It is therefore not unusual to walk different puppies that are distantly related. There have been a couple of occasions where I have recognised traits or characteristics that have reminded me of a previous puppy, only to discover that the two are distantly related. My next pup, Varley, was one of these.

Varley was a chunky pup with stocky legs and very pale hair, and reminded me very much of Errol. So much so that I mentioned it to my supervisor, now Sam, when she came for her first visit, and asked if she knew whether they were related. The breeding programme is very carefully monitored and recorded to ensure there is no in-breeding, and my supervisor was easily able to check his pedigree. She soon discovered he was related to Errol on his father's side. I was pleased that my observations had been correct.

I soon discovered that looks were not all that Varley had inherited. Not only did he look like Errol, but in the house he behaved like him. Furniture and toys were chewed and food stolen. All the experience that we had had with Errol was coming to the fore. Shoes and clothes were removed to high

Varley

places and, after the loss of his favourite jumper, Mark had become an expert at remembering to keep his bedroom door shut.

It was a different story when I wanted to walk him outside the house, and at this point any similarities Varley had to his notorious relative Errol ceased. Any confidence he had vanished instantly, and he would begin to show signs of complete stress. As we walked down the gravel drive towards the road his insecurities would set in straight away, and his reluctance to go anywhere would turn to panic as we reached the end of the drive and turned onto the pavement. Varley would hold the lead in his mouth or he would jump up at me. His eyes would grow bigger and he would have a look of panic on his face. Guide dogs are not allowed to walk holding the lead in their mouth, but if I stopped him he would bite my skirt or trouser legs or jacket. Soon, many of my clothes had small tears in them from where Varley had grabbed them while we were walking, or rather trying to walk, somewhere.

Every time I tried to walk Varley I decided to think positively that he was going to be all right that day, in the hope that it would affect his attitude, but to no avail. I tried everything I could think of to make walking a pleasant and non-scary experience for him. I eventually discovered that he would walk without jumping, biting and chewing if we were in VERY quiet areas where there was no traffic noise, not even in the distance. My most successful area to walk Varley was a quiet housing estate in Twyford. I had to drive there, park the car and then walk round the few roads – not very exciting, but at least he walked. It was the only place where he walked like a normal dog. Anywhere else was a challenge, even coaxing him with his favourite toys such as a small teddy bear or a ball on a rope didn't result in any success. With my previous puppies the 'year' had gone quickly, but with Varley it was a long twelve months.

Most dogs are happy to walk on the lead on pavements and in built-up areas, and a free run in a field or a wood is usually the icing on the cake, but Varley didn't even enjoy a free run. When I took him to the field area near my house we would travel in the car so that he didn't have to experience the worry of the busy road, then I would open the back of the car so that he could go free running into the field. Once out of the car he would go about five yards away from me and then come back with his tail between his legs. If I put his lead back on him, then he would walk in a relaxed manner. After trying to walk him in a wide variety of different places – the fields by the railway track, the footpath alongside the river, the woods near my friends' houses, the local park and even the quiet, unmade-up gravel road down to the river – I began to see a pattern. It seemed that outside noise, in particular from traffic, was the trigger that made him anxious.

Varley was rapidly turning into the most difficult pup that I had walked so far. I found myself ringing Sam for advice several times between visits – something that I had really only had to do when my dog had had health problems up until that point. I was beginning to wonder if I could continue to walk him for the whole year and was already certain that there was no way he was going to make it as a guide dog. Sam was sympathetic to my situation. She even asked if I would like her to rehome him. "No, I'll struggle on with him as long as you will back me up," I said. "Oh, that's good," was the reply, "because if you can't cope, I don't know who else to give him to." Was this a compliment?

Varley's general health and fitness were good, but he did have some problems with his eyes. After we had had Varley for a few weeks I started to notice that his eyes were always red. I took him to the vet to get them checked out. She looked closely at his eyes and identified the problem as ectropion. This is a condition where the lower eyelids fall away from the eyeballs and don't touch them at all. This must have been very uncomfortable for him, particularly in wet and windy weather, and may well have contributed to his unwillingness to walk.

One day, to see how he must have been feeling, I decided to try walking with my lower eyelids pulled away from my eyes. I gently pulled my lower lids away from my eyeballs and started walking down the pavement. In a short space of time my eyes became very dry and painful, and I had to quickly let my bottom eyelids go back to where they belonged, something Varley couldn't do. I had also been walking quite slowly, but a dog would walk faster, especially on a free run, which would have exacerbated the problem. After having done my little experiment I was much more sympathetic to his condition. Veterinary science, just like medicine, is continually advancing, and there are many more treatments and operations available to the dogs than there used to be. When Varley was fully grown and in the training centre, he had an operation on his eyes which rectified the problem. This must have helped him considerably.

Varley was a difficult dog in all areas of life. He wasn't totally happy being in a car either. He would bark continually when I was filling the car with petrol and he would bark all the time if I left him alone in the car. Travelling in the well of the passenger seat seemed to be the place where he was most relaxed and so, instead of travelling in the back of the car like all my dogs before or since, he was allowed to travel there. He was definitely a complex dog with issues.

I found my year of walking Varley very hard. He was naughty in the house and didn't like walking. Puppies don't usually have both problems. A lively pup in the house can be taken out for a good working walk to get rid of the surplus energy. On the other hand, a pup that isn't too happy walking is not often a destructive dog in the house. With Varley I was in a no-win situation. Added to all this was the health problem he had with his eyes. In all areas – working, playing, being a pet and health-wise – he had difficulties. Varley continued to challenge me right up to the day he went for training. The weekend before he went, we had friends coming to stay and I was busy preparing an evening meal. Chris called me to check on something in the garden, and I was only gone for a few minutes, but by the time I returned to the kitchen Varley had eaten most of the lasagne that I had been preparing. Looking at his face I am sure he enjoyed it. That was the straw that broke the camel's back. I asked my supervisor if she could collect him a day earlier than originally planned, which she did. Varley was not going to be able to come back if he needed a career change – which my supervisor Sam and I were both certain would happen. Even so, I did shed a few tears for him when he went as I didn't think kennel life was going to suit him either.

My fears were realised. Poor Varley wasn't happy in kennels. He was not cut out to be a guide dog. He was operated on to correct his ectropion but this didn't affect his reaction to noise and his reluctance to walk anywhere but in quiet places. As we had expected, he needed a career change. Guide Dogs holds a list of people who would like to offer a home to these dogs, and the rehoming officer takes as much care in finding new owners that match the dogs' needs and personalities as the training staff do in matching working dogs with their owners. Varley's needs were very unusual and he was rehomed with a lady who had about three acres of land. There he could run free and enjoy himself without having to cope with any traffic noise or leave the house where he felt safe and comfortable. At last he had landed on his feet, although it took him several months before he relaxed completely. We had given the rehoming officer permission to pass on our contact details to his new owner should they wish to get in touch with us. It was a few months later that I received a phone call from her, Shirley, inviting us to visit him. She had given him a new name to go with his new lifestyle. He was now known as Barley, just a variation on his original name so easy for him to adjust to. He was also lucky to be able to share his new home with Oliver, an animal rescue dog. Shirley's main worry was that Barley was putting on weight very rapidly. She was reducing the amount of food she was giving him, but it seemed to make no difference. He must have been a happy, relaxed dog with her.

David and I arrived at Barley's new home in my old, brown, Mini Clubman estate, the car that he had ridden in when with us as a pup. He recognised the sound of it and ran to meet us. As soon as the engine had stopped David opened his passenger door to stroke Barley, but he had other ideas. He was so pleased to see us that he jumped straight into the car onto David and me. There isn't too much room in the front of a Mini but there is considerably less when it is shared with an eighty-pound Labrador. It was great to see Barley so happy and so loved.

12

Falcon, the water lover

The most successful breed of dog for a guide dog is the Labrador crossed with a golden retriever. They seem to have the happy mix of an enthusiastic Labrador and the more stubborn personality of the retriever. Having had a challenging time with Varley I was ready for a different puppy. It was good to get Falcon, a Labrador crossed with a golden retriever and a much easier pup to train. From the moment he arrived I could tell that I was in for a much less challenging time than I had had with his predecessor.

Falcon walked confidently into the house and had a good sniff around under the island bench in the middle of the kitchen and all around the cupboards

Falcon as a pup

at the edge. He was quickly introduced to Lynton, who refused to play – he always did when a new pup arrived. This changed once he had established his senior position. Falcon understood that Lynton was top dog, automatically giving him the doggy respect he deserved. He was friendly, fun, calm and quiet in the house – a big change from my previous experience.

Within a couple of days Falcon was ready for a walk out of the house and garden. When puppies arrive at six to seven weeks old they have never worn a collar and lead. One of the first jobs of the puppy-walker is to put a collar on them. Quite a challenge to do with such a fluffy, wriggly animal. I solve the problem by waiting until the puppy is in a deep sleep and then gently putting on the collar. When he wakes up he is curious about whatever is around his neck, has a good scratch, but is totally unaware that I was the culprit who put it there.

After a couple of days of wearing a collar, Falcon and I were ready to try a little walk along the pavement to the post box at the end of the road – a distance of about 200 yards. I attached the lead onto Falcon's collar and we set off. He did really well. A bit of zigzagging to inspect all the new sights and smells, but otherwise he was a confident little walker – a complete contrast to Varley. He needed to be carried a few times, a total of 400 yards is a long way at seven weeks old, but even then he could experience everything that was going on in the outside world, including some 'Ahs!' and 'Isn't he cute!' from passers-by that we met. This was much more what I had come to expect of a guide dog puppy and already I was looking forward to my year with Falcon. He was well-behaved in the house and was easy to walk on the lead. Perfect, or almost perfect. He did have two weak areas: first, he was easily led by other pups, and second, he loved water.

When he was with me, or Lynton, who by this time was back with us as a pet, Falcon was very well-behaved. He obeyed my commands and copied Lynton's good behaviour. Things were a little bit different when we were in the company of other dogs who were a little more adventurous.

It was Falcon who took part in the mini-riot with my friend's pup that was silenced by Lynton's bark when travelling in the back of her car.

Most water-loving dogs, when free running, are happy to run through puddles and splash about in them. Falcon's approach was different. He would rush towards the water with his head lowered and his bottom jaw in the water. He then carried on running through the water, blowing bubbles and producing bow waves either side of him. The first time he did this he was on a lead and we were walking along an unmade-up road; it took me by surprise and I burst out laughing. At this stage, I realised he would have to give up this behaviour when he was a working guide dog, although he could probably get away with it when on a free run. I became very particular about free run areas. Clean puddles were acceptable, but the muddy ones were his favourite and not mine. His ability to sniff out water was incredible. He would have found a muddy puddle in a desert.

Falcon went into training at a year old and sailed through with no major glitches. His love of water didn't cause him any problems when working, and before long he had qualified as a guide dog. Not long after he qualified I received a phone call from his owner. Trainers take great care to match their dogs with their owners. In this case they had also managed to cater for the dog's idiosyncrasies. I'm not sure it had been done deliberately but, luckily

Falcon and the bow wave

for Falcon, his guide dog owner lived in an area that was prone to flooding – more water than even he could have asked for.

When free running, Falcon's owner allowed him to have fun in the puddles – the deeper and muddier the better as far as he was concerned. On a good day he could be covered in mud on his face, legs, underneath and sides. Only a thin strip of clean dry hair would be left on his back. The penalty for this behaviour was a bath followed by a blow dry with a hairdryer – a price he was quite prepared to pay. A guide dog on the lead is very much at work. Once out for a free run, though, they change into fun-filled pets where all their individual characteristics come out in full.

Handsome Hobo
and the tortoises

My tenth pup was my first golden retriever and was called Hobo – one of my favourite names for a puppy. He was another easy-going puppy and a pleasure to walk. Fortunately, he didn't show any of the self-willed characteristics for which goldies have a reputation. It was during the time we were walking Hobo that David's interest in animals began to escalate and the number of pets in our garden increased.

Following the deaths of my father one week before Hobo arrived and my mother two years earlier, there were three pets which needed to be rehomed. My aunt adopted Lyn, their black scruffy-looking cairn terrier, and we gave a home to their two battered-looking tortoises. As it was November, we had to wait until the spring to bring our new pets home because they were hibernating in my father's much-loved garden, under the beech hedge in a cosy den that he had made for them. My parents had owned these two animals for at least thirty years. Both had been found at different times by concerned neighbours who didn't want them but knew that my parents had owned tortoises in the past and sent them their way. The tortoises were never claimed and so they spent their lives roaming free in my parents' large garden.

For reasons unbeknown to me they were always just 'the tortoises' and had never been given names. I think perhaps that by the time it was obvious that no one was going to claim them 'the tortoises' had just stuck as a name, with one being distinguished from the other by its size. Naming the two animals was now a priority job, not that we had any hope of them coming when they were called – and tortoises gave us a whole new raft of names to consider. After much debate we called the male, which was the larger of the two, Tornado and the smaller female we named Hurricane. We also have a large garden and the tortoises were allowed to roam free there once we'd checked the fences had no holes they could escape through.

The tortoises, Hurricane and Tornado

Tortoises are known for being slow animals, but it is amazing how easy it is to lose them when you turn your back for a few minutes. They are, however, creatures of habit, and once Tornado and Hurricane had settled into their new surroundings they could usually be found in one of half a dozen areas in the garden. Hurricane's favourite bed was in the compost heap – an area at the far corner of the garden where old fence panels had been used to make the sides and rear of a row of three containers in which the vegetable matter was dumped. One was used for current rubbish, one was rotting down and the third was used for composting the garden. Hurricane would climb up the open end of the completely rotted section and burrow about twelve inches into the warm rotting compost until she was completely hidden. Tornado, on the other hand, took the easy option and usually clambered over the wooden doorframe and trundled to the warmest corner of the greenhouse, making himself a shallow pit in the soil to sleep in. On a really lazy day he wouldn't even bother with the effort involved in making the pit, but instead would park himself in the large cardboard box with straw in it that had been left lying on its side in the greenhouse.

We soon discovered that two tortoises roaming free in the garden could cause a few problems. I was happy for them to eat a few weeds, especially dandelions and clover in the lawn, but not plants in our vegetable patch. They had other ideas and went to great lengths to access the succulent young shoots that appeared when the vegetables started growing through. Pea guards were essential to protect young plants in the vegetable patch, otherwise a row of young beans and peas would be eaten in a day. Leeks and onions were quite safe as neither tortoise considered them to be a delicacy. My much-loved flower-beds were also at risk from the tortoises, ice plant (sedum), alstroemeria and foxgloves being among their favourites. After their initial feasting on my carefully cultivated flowers I decided that I needed pea guards there to protect my most 'tortoise vulnerable' plants. They didn't add to the beauty of the flower-bed, but it did mean that at least I had some flowers to look at.

Although our tortoises roamed free and picked their own food out of the garden, I did give them treats. They especially liked watery salad stuffs and fruit – lettuce, cucumber, tomatoes, strawberries and raspberries – and so I would save them the end pieces that we cut off when preparing salads. Tortoises don't have teeth but a razor sharp edge to their jaws instead, so hand-feeding has to be done with care. They open their jaws very wide, put their heads forward and bite onto the food. This results in a V-shaped portion being taken out of the lettuce, cucumber, etc. They can't really see what they are aiming at as their eyes are quite high up on the sides of their faces, so if the piece of food is quite small, they can easily bite the fingers holding it. There is no way you can pull your finger out – believe me, I have tried. However, after a couple of seconds' delay, while the animal is registering that the finger is not a tasty treat, it will open its jaw again and release the trapped finger. No blood will have been drawn but there is a very marked, rather painful, red V-shaped mark left on the skin. It really is a case of once bitten, twice shy.

One summer as I was out walking the puppy I saw a notice in our local shop window: 'Found, one tortoise'. I read all the details and was really interested that we weren't the only people in the road to have this unusual pet. When I got home I looked for Hurricane and Tornado. Tornado was there but I couldn't find Hurricane. I looked in all her normal patches but couldn't see her. In fact, I couldn't remember seeing her at all for the previous three or four days. That was nothing unusual, as tortoises don't get up until it is warm enough for them to heat up, and they go to bed before the temperature drops too much; after all, they are solar powered. I was beginning to get suspicious; maybe the 'found' tortoise didn't belong to someone else but was in fact mine.

I phoned the number on the 'found' notice. The person who answered had found a tortoise and described it as looking a bit like a battered German helmet. I mentioned a couple of Hurricane's other features, such as a missing claw, and we agreed that it was probably my tortoise. They lived about six doors down the road from us but, unfortunately, Hurricane was no longer with them as she had escaped from the box she had been put in. But there was good news – she had been found by their next-door neighbours, eating their lettuces, and they had put her in their greenhouse. This time she hadn't managed to escape and I went round to collect her, taking the cat travel cage to put her safely in, and brought her home. Before letting her out to roam again I checked the fencing all round our garden, especially in the areas where it was hidden by large bushes and shrubs, but couldn't find anywhere that she could have escaped through. She regained her freedom of the garden.

The next day I found her coming out of our garage and heading through another door towards our driveway and the road. To get to the garage she had had to climb two brick steps up to the patio and then go through the door on the side of the covered way in front of the garage, which had been left open by mistake. This must have been her escape route a few days earlier when the main garage door to the front drive was open. The people who had found her lived about one hundred yards down the road from us and she had been found purposefully walking around their front garden. I was once again surprised by the speed and tenacity of these animals that, up until now, I had always considered to be slow and uninteresting as pets. Hurricane and Tornado were definitely proving themselves otherwise.

Every year Hurricane laid about six eggs, usually in June. This was when she got the wanderlust and became much more adventurous. This must have been the reason for her setting off to pastures new when the opportunity arose. Another year, neighbours at the end of our garden came to ask if we had lost a tortoise because they had found one in their garden. That time she had burrowed under a slightly rotten part of the fence to make her escape.

Our tortoises hibernated every winter from about early October. Originally we put Hurricane and Tornado back in the dens that my father had made under the beech hedge, but later on we put them in cardboard boxes with dry soil at the bottom and straw on the top, then kept the tortoises in a cold but frost-free area either in the garage or under our covered sideway. One year, the weather changed very suddenly from warm and sunny to cold and wet. I went to collect Hurricane and Tornado from the garden to hibernate them. I found Tornado quickly, but there was no sign of Hurricane. We looked in all her favourite hiding places but with no luck. I couldn't see her in the compost heap either. I was quite sad at the thought that we might lose her over winter, especially as she was my favourite. I hoped that her good sense of survival and self-preservation would stand her in good stead for surviving a cold winter. We also did all we could to help her if she had hibernated herself. We decided not to use the compost that winter just in case she was in there, and we didn't dig up any plants in areas where she sometimes slept just in case she had buried herself under them. Then we crossed our fingers and waited to see what would happen.

About six months later, on a lovely spring day, I met Hurricane walking up the garden path towards me. She looked as if she had had a really good sleep and was glad to be alive on such a lovely day. I was delighted to see her and met her with: "Hello! Am I pleased to see you!" Then realised I was talking to a tortoise and hoped the neighbours hadn't heard me.

Hobo took the additional pets in his stride, happy to live in harmony with all of them – tortoises, chickens, quails, Lynton, and Miffy the cat – ideal behaviour from a guide dog pup. He did get ruffled on a couple of occasions. He was not happy when another dog wanted to share his dinner, nor when another puppy wanted his toy. We worked on these things, but they would prove to be his downfall in later life.

Hobo qualified quickly, went to work with a lady in Portsmouth and was a much-loved, handsome guide dog. He came to stay with us for a couple of weeks while she was on holiday. It's really lovely to look after an ex-pupil, but also a responsibility. I am always aware of how much time, effort and money has gone into training them to this level but also of the strong bond that there always is between the guide dog and its owner.

While he was with us we took Hobo on all his favourite walks, and it was on one of these outings that we met trouble. Hobo was attacked by a local dog, a young boxer. It bit his ear and hung on, and it was several seconds before he let go, with poor Hobo crying all the time. It was one of those occasions where my heart was in my mouth as I watched the scene unfold but, until the boxer let go, there was nothing I could do. The result was a puncture wound which became infected and needed a course of antibiotics to cure the injury.

This incident must have made a lasting impression on Hobo and sometime later when he was working, walking with his owner down their local high street, he decided to give vent to his feelings on a passing dog, another boxer. No damage was done but the incident had to be reported to Guide Dogs staff, and it was decided to retire Hobo at this stage before anything more serious happened. This was a great pity as he was only five years old at the time and a good guide dog that should have been able to work for several more years. Hobo's owner asked if I would have him as a retired dog but, much as I had a soft spot for him, I still wanted to puppy-walk. His attitude would not have been a good example to a trainee puppy so I had to say no.

14

Don't count
your chickens

The next addition to our growing menagerie was a number of small chickens, bantams to be precise. My cousin Mervyn had a farm with bantams free running and, having heard that David would like some, promised him some chicks from the next hatching. In anticipation of their arrival, Chris and Dave built our first chicken house. It was made from old, six-foot square, larch lap fence panels. They needed some work done on them to replace the rotten slats at their base but were soon sturdy enough to be made into an A-frame chicken house. Two panels formed the sides of the A, while other panels were cut into two triangles and nailed to an A-shaped frame to make the two end panels. One of these end panels had a nest box in it, while the other had a pop-hole to let the bantams go in and out of the house. The whole of this end panel could also be easily removed so that David could get into the house to clean it out. The floor was made of reasonably sturdy old floorboards and there were two perches inside. All we needed now were our bantams.

It seemed ages before Mervyn phoned to say he had some chicks for David. As soon as we could after the phone call, we went to collect them. There were four chicks and they were four weeks old. It's difficult to sex young chicks so, as we didn't want four cockerels, Mervyn agreed that we could bring back any cocks. We left the farm with a cardboard box containing four young chicks and an excited son eagerly staring in at them through the top of the box as we drove home.

We had an inauspicious start to our lives as poultry keepers as on our next visit to the farm we had to explain that one of the chicks had died and the others were probably cocks. Not entirely unexpected as, generally speaking, a brood of chicks will always contain more cocks than hens. There were no more chicks for us to have at the time, but there was a black and white speckled bantam about the same age as ours running around the farm.

David was told that, if he could catch it, he could have it. It was probably a hen, although opinions were divided. David had no problem catching the bird, so she came home with us. On the way back we were trying to think of a name for her. We came through a village en route called Hartley Wintney, so we decided to call her Hartley.

We introduced Hartley to our other bantams, who were not very pleased to see her on their patch and began chasing her around the garden. We were sitting on a low wall around the edge of our fish pond, watching their antics and ready to sort out any major fights. Hartley decided to come to us for protection and hopped up onto the wall and stood between us. Soon, Hartley was becoming quite a tame bird, would come when called and would quite happily let us pick her up. We were also rapidly coming to the conclusion that 'she' was probably a 'he'. Four cocks and no hens was not quite what we wanted, so they were going to have to go back to the farm. Well, three were going back, but Hartley had wormed his way into our affections and was allowed to stay. We just hoped that our neighbours would not object to a bantam cock living next door. One neighbour said he had no objection but did ask what he was called, as he reminded him of a cockerel he had heard every morning while on a holiday in France.

Hartley proved to be quite a character. Despite having a designer house to sleep in, every night he would perch on the branch of a tree, which overhung the chicken house. The branch was about eight feet high, too high for us to reach him. So, every night David used a garden fork to lift him off his branch. He would gently put the handle under Hartley's chest, Hartley would step up onto the fork and then David would carefully lower him down and put him onto the perch in the chicken house out of harm's way. He became very tame. If we whistled and called him he would come running. He was quite happy to eat corn out of our hands. He would also perch on our arms and be carried round the garden – did he think he was a parrot?!

David and Hartley

We have a compost heap at the end of the garden. Anyone taking vegetable peelings to the compost heap would call Hartley and he would happily follow them all the way. This expedition became known as the 'Hartley Run' and to this day, although there is no Hartley around, taking peelings to the compost heap is still known as 'Doing the Hartley Run'.

Apart from being tame, he was quite intelligent – for a chicken. Inspired by the television programme *Bird Brain of Britain*, David tested Hartley's brain power by building a structure out of Lego. There were four tasks that Hartley had to do to get some corn and they had to be done in a particular order to release the food. First he had to open a chute to release the corn into a little Lego trolley, then pull the trolley by the string attached to it along a 'tunnel' to a closed door. He opened this door by pulling a third piece of string, allowing the trolley to roll to a second door which he opened by pulling a final piece of string. At last, out came the trolley and Hartley could eat the corn it contained. Quite clever, don't you think?

Having a tame bantam had some disadvantages. If we left the back door or patio doors open, Hartley would pop in to see us. It was a bit disconcerting when watching the television to see a cockerel walk into the room, especially as he had to come through the utility room, kitchen and hall to get to us.

Although Hartley was a splendid pet, we still didn't have any chickens that laid eggs. As a consolation, friends gave Dave five female Coturnix quails that were surplus to their requirements. They are about the same size as a thrush and have similar markings, but are much rounder birds, rather like the shape of a robin on a Christmas card. David used a guinea pig hutch with an enclosed run to house these birds. Within a couple of hours of arriving they had laid eggs. Not in the hutch, but anywhere they liked in the grass run. Things were no better at bedtime, as the birds stayed outside in the grass run and had no intention of going to bed in the hutch. This meant that every night, for their safety, we had to catch them and put them in their sleeping quarters. Quails aren't very tame birds, so even catching them was a challenge. As egg-layers, they were worth their weight in gold but, compared with them as pets, Hartley was an outright winner.

David soon made a more suitable house and run for the quails. It was basically a large run covered in small gauge chicken wire. One third was the sleeping area with a wooden floor, a waterproofed hinged roof and three sides made of wood. The fourth side was wire netting covered with heavy duty, clear polythene which let some light into the sleeping area. This was what we thought they needed, but it was not one hundred per cent successful because, although the birds laid most of their eggs in the house, they still preferred to sleep under the stars and had to be put to bed each night.

We kept the run on the lawn and put a seed tray with garden soil in it so they could have a dust bath. Sometimes we put the whole run on an area of the vegetable patch with some weeds on it, to make their lives more exciting. We also gave up putting them to bed each night, a decision which later turned out to be fatal. We soon discovered that a six-foot-high wooden fence was no deterrent to a hungry fox. I went down the garden one Sunday morning to discover feathers on the lawn, a large hole under the run and no quails to be seen anywhere. Although quails were not our favourite pets, they were a valuable part of our menagerie for two to three years, mostly due to their egg production. However, it did need sixteen quail eggs to make an omelette for the family, each one carefully cut open with a pair of scissors.

In addition to being given adult female quails, David was later given fertile quail eggs. He was lent an incubator to hatch them in and given instructions on what to do. We bought a book about keeping quails which gave us a lot of useful information. There are three main requirements for hatching eggs in an incubator: 1) a constant temperature, 2) the correct humidity and 3) regularly keeping the eggs turned. The incubator that we were lent didn't turn the eggs automatically so David had to turn them manually twice a day. He also had to check the water level to keep up the humidity and to make sure the temperature remained steady. He must have done a really good job as we had twenty eggs and eighteen of them hatched. Day-old quails are striped black and yellow, look like bumble bees and are not a lot bigger.

Twenty-four hours after hatching, we put them in a brooder, another piece of home-made equipment. This was a large glass fish tank with newspaper and sawdust in the bottom, and a ventilated lid on the top which had some electric cable going through it holding a red 60-watt light bulb about two inches above the quails' heads. This kept the birds warm without being too bright for their eyes. Every day we raised the bulb about an inch (a clothes peg kept the bulb at the right height). When it reached the top, we changed the bulb for a lower strength one, 40-watt, then 25-watt, and repeated the height adjustment every day. The quails ran around the fish tank, eating, drinking and sleeping. If the temperature dropped too low, they huddled under the light. When this happened we had to either lower the bulb or put a stronger one back in to increase the temperature. As they grew, we moved them to a wooden hutch with two compartments. The sleeping area still had an electric light bulb to heat it, but the other area remained unheated. The hutch was kept in the covered, enclosed area adjoining the side of our house. When they were five to six weeks old they were big enough to go into the hutch and run in the garden.

David incubated several batches of quails' eggs, with a very high success rate. We eventually bought our own incubator, which had an automatic turner, making hatching eggs much more reliable. Even with this better incubator, my one attempt to hatch eggs was a complete failure. I forgot to keep the water topped up, so the eggs dried up and not one chick hatched. At this point I decided to leave David or a broody hen to do the job.

Norton, Nero and the feathered menagerie

"What is that dog barking at now?" I hadn't thought there were so many scary things in the world. But there he was: tail down, hackles up, trying to be brave, but deep down inside he was scared, something that seemed to happen on a daily basis with this latest puppy.

Norton, a yellow Labrador crossed with a golden retriever, found our ever increasing menagerie of animals more difficult to cope with than Hobo had. At first he thought the flighty bantams were good fun to chase and in no time at all was battering the carefully pruned shrubs in the border as he followed them through the flower-bed, so we had to stop him doing that very quickly. The tortoises were a different matter. A stone that walked was quite scary, so his answer to the problem was to stand about two yards away and bark. Try as I might, there was no way I could convince him that they weren't a threat so, after half an hour of constant barking, I gave up and put him indoors in the utility room. It was days before he decided to accept them as part of the family.

Tortoises weren't the only thing Norton had an issue with. Virtually anything different, unusual or out of his experience meant he resorted to a prolonged session of loud and frantic barking. On refuse collection mornings in particular we had very noisy walks. Outside every house on the grass verge was a collection of overflowing recycling bins, black polythene bags of rubbish and dustbins of all shapes and sizes, and they were a big problem to him. It took several weeks of early Monday morning walks around the local roads, stopping to bark at the piles of rubbish we passed, to get him used to them. I even took to putting different random objects, such as a large brightly coloured garden chair or an old garden fork, on our lawn every day to help him conquer his fears. Most items were barked at initially and then barked at again before being deemed harmless. For this behaviour, he acquired the title 'Noisy, Naughty Norton'.

I wasn't sure, with all his fears, whether or not he would qualify. You can't have a qualified guide dog stop in the middle of guiding his owner to work to have a quick bark at something new they have just encountered. However, with much work and careful training, Norton qualified and was much loved by his owner, who rang me to tell me how delighted he was with his dog. Norton wasn't a natural as a guide dog and the job proved to be too hard for him. He was retired after nine months and rehomed as a pet.

Norton had gone and I was beginning to remember what it was like to have a quieter household where everything didn't need to be barked at, when I had a phone call from my supervisor at 10am on a Monday morning. "Would you like to have another male golden retriever?" The dog, whose name was Nelson, was already on his way from the breeding centre in Warwickshire to Wokingham where they had been expecting one called Nellie, who was due to be placed with a 'bitches only' puppy-walker. I agreed, but said the name Nelson would be a problem for me. I didn't want another dog whose name ended in 'on' because whenever I had disciplined Falcon or Norton, Lynton, now my pet German Shepherd, a sensitive dog, felt he was in trouble as well. So it was agreed that I could change Nelson's name as long as it began with 'N'. Nigel was suggested as an alternative, but as we had a couple of friends with that name, I went for Nero. So it was that puppy number twelve arrived with very little notice – about three hours.

At 1pm I drove up the long tarmac drive that led to the Guide Dogs Centre at Wokingham. The centre had been paid for by money collected in a *Blue Peter* Appeal, and driving up to fetch Nero I had my usual feelings of anticipation about this new pup.

Nero was a very pretty puppy, but I soon discovered he had a couple of health problems. The main one was digestive. Within a few days of Nero's arrival I was visiting the vet with him following a bout of diarrhoea. He was diagnosed with colitis and given a seven-day course of antibiotics. This solved his problem for two to three weeks, but then his symptoms returned and another course of antibiotics was needed. This turned out to be a long-term problem, and Nero was eight months old before his colitis was under control.

Nero's other problem was dandruff, which I didn't notice at first as his pale skin and hair masked it. I did notice white flakes on the utility room floor when I swept it, but assumed I had spilt some washing powder. I suddenly realised where the white specks were coming from when I gave him a cuddle wearing a black mohair cardigan. When I put him back into his basket I found I was covered in a dusting of small, white specks. A careful inspection of his skin underneath the hair showed me the reason: dandruff. It was a good job Nero was a pale golden retriever and not a black dog. Until he was better I was very conscious of what colour clothes I wore.

Apart from his ongoing health problems and frequent visits to the vet, Nero slotted into our lifestyle very quickly and built up a good rapport with all our pets. Hartley became his special friend and they soon began to play together. It wasn't long before Hartley had taught Nero how to play-fight – or was it the other way around? Each game followed the same format.

First of all, they faced each other, and Nero did a play bow; that is, head lowered, front legs down on the ground and bottom still in the air. Hartley responded in a similar way – head down and bottom in the air and, as he didn't have any front legs, he spread his wings wide on the ground either side of his body. After staring at each other in this position for a few seconds, they pivoted around until they were side by side and then kept nudging each other.

Then they returned to their original positions facing each other, ready for the attack. Nero went up on his hind legs and pushed Hartley with his front legs. Hartley, on the other hand, came in with all guns blazing, using his outstretched wings to grab Nero, while jumping up and kicking Nero with the soles of his feet. The end result was both animals on

Hartley and Nero, beginning of the play-fight

the ground. Sometimes Nero had Hartley pinned to the floor but, in most cases, Hartley was the winner and had Nero on his back, pinned to the ground.

I was concerned for the safety of both animals since Hartley's sharp claws could have scratched Nero and drawn blood, while, although only eight weeks old, Nero was already two to three times heavier than the bantam cock. The play-fighting challenges continued until Nero left us at one year old, despite many attempts by me to stop them. The two animals enjoyed their regular playtimes and there never was any damage to either of them, which was fortunate as the fights were now between a featherweight three-pound bantam and a super-heavyweight seventy-pound golden retriever.

Nero was good with all the birds in the garden. Our quails, which were not the tamest of birds, periodically flew out of their run when I collected their eggs. They weren't great fliers and usually skimmed across the vegetable patch to take shelter under a cabbage or some other vegetable. As I went to pick them up, they took off and landed a few feet away under another plant – a no-win situation for me. This is where Nero scored maximum Brownie points. He was brilliant at finding a quail amongst the vegetation, catching it with the body in his mouth and the head sticking out to one side. When he found a bird I could call him to me and, after about a minute, he would gently place the still fit and healthy quail in my hands. He saved me hours of time walking in circles around the veg patch.

Vikki, Hereford and Hampshire were our first bantam hens. They were about four months old when they were given to David by an assistant in the shop where we bought our hay, straw and chicken feed. They were no particular breed and each had different markings, making them easy to identify. Vikki was all black, Hereford was black but with brown speckled feathers on her neck and Hampshire was all white. Hereford and Hampshire kept our theme of place names and fitted in well with Hartley, giving a slight *My Fair Lady* connection.

To Hartley they were his 'fair ladies' and he was very proud of his little harem. He really looked

Hartley and his fair ladies

after them and was the perfect gentleman. All four bantams ran free around the garden, and whenever Hartley found anything good to eat he would let out a loud call to the three hens to come over and share the food he had found, never eating any himself until they had arrived and begun eating. Now he had divided loyalties between us and his hens.

It was a couple of months after Vikki, Hereford and Hampshire arrived that we got our first egg. I realised one day as I was watching them that Vikki's comb was very red, the sign of a laying chicken. She then disappeared from view, and it wasn't long before I also heard the familiar sound of a hen that had just laid an egg – about four short clucks followed by one longer one which goes up in pitch, which is repeated several times. David and I rushed to check the nest box and to our excitement we found three eggs. And so I began my habit of writing in pencil on the shell the date each egg was laid. This way I could be sure to use the eggs in the order they were collected.

Years, and many eggs, later I still get great pleasure from collecting eggs from the nest box and always make some comment like, "Well done, girls." We also have a few friends who will ask if they can go and collect eggs when they come. Visiting children always want to do that job, so I make a big effort to make sure they will not be disappointed. So far, no one has noticed that sometimes they collect an egg that has a date written on it in pencil.

After a few months we bought three brown hens to add to our brood: Speckle, Beaky and Saffron, who were cross-breed, what I call basic, egg-laying chickens. They reliably laid in the nest box one egg per chicken each day and, unlike the bantams, they continued to lay eggs all through the winter. Most pure-bred chickens moult in the autumn and go 'off lay' until the early spring. They were very tame birds and came when they were called. They would also eat corn out of our hands and let us pick them up. Perhaps Hartley had influenced their behaviour? These three were the first of a succession of hens, but none were quite as tame or such good layers as these first three birds.

Close neighbours also had a small menagerie of rabbits, guinea pigs, chickens and ducks. We often compared notes and went to them for advice on what to do with our chickens. They too liked to incubate eggs, and it wasn't long before we acquired a pair of ducks which they had hatched. They were Silver Appleyards, a breed which had originally been bred from mallards and were a similar size. The female was all white and we called her Jemima – from the *Tale of Jemima Puddle-Duck*. The drake had markings similar to a mallard and he was called Desmond – the name of the duck in the *Captain Beaky* verses.

Ducks love water and ours needed a pond. Knowing the damage ducks can do to water plants, and being rather proud of our large pond with its selection of water lilies, iris and goldfish, I was not prepared for them to share and destroy it. They would need a pond of their own. David dug a large hole about six feet in diameter and two to three feet deep in the chicken run, as far away from the apple trees as he could, to prevent it filling with fallen leaves. He lined it with butyl rubber, and as soon as it was filled with water the ducks were in there swimming. Most of their day was spent on the pond, either swimming or 'duck diving'. Whichever they did, they did it together. They would have been good contenders for a synchronised swimming competition. They loved the water, and the phrase 'like a duck takes to water' took on a real meaning seeing how much they flourished in their little pond.

One Sunday morning in December I decided to feed all the animals and let them out before going to church. When I got home about two hours later David was rather concerned about the whereabouts of Jemima and Desmond as he couldn't find them anywhere. I could remember seeing them when I let them out of their house, but there was certainly no sign of them now – not even a pile of feathers indicating a visit from the fox. We printed several notes to put in neighbours' letter boxes asking if anyone had seen a pair of ducks and giving a contact telephone number. Within a couple of hours, we had a phone call from a neighbour who lived about 200 yards away from us to say that one duck was in his back garden. We rushed to collect it and bring it home. It was Desmond, who was disorientated but otherwise fit and well, but there was no sign of Jemima.

At 7am the following morning we had a phone call, "Are you the people who have lost a duck? There is an injured one in the gutter about halfway down your road." We rushed out, unsure of what to expect, and found Jemima about thirty yards from our house lying at the side of the road looking very sorry for herself. She had a cut with blood oozing from the side of her face, wasn't moving and seemed dazed. She didn't try to fly away from us as we carefully picked her up and laid her in a towel to carry her home.

Immediately, part of the utility room was sectioned off as an intensive care unit for Jemima the patient. We found an old fireguard that we had used when the children were young and put it against the wall of the utility room. We put newspaper on the floor, gave her a bowl of water to drink and put the central heating boiler on – a pampered pet. We cleaned her face but could see no other damage. We kept her indoors and took her to the vet the next day. Apart from the cut on Jemima's face, the vet could find nothing else wrong with her. To prevent an infection setting in, he prescribed a course of antibiotics and then we brought Jemima home to her improvised intensive care ward.

The medication was in liquid form so that it could be added to her drinking water. We mixed the right amount of water and antibiotic and put it in a heavy duty dog water bowl so that she didn't knock it over. Unfortunately, Jemima was refusing to eat or drink anything and just sat quietly on the floor. Meanwhile, at the end of the garden, there was a distraught drake, Desmond. He too was not eating or drinking and spent the whole day walking up and down by the fence. They were obviously pining for each other so I decided the only solution was to bring Desmond to Jemima and let him share her intensive care facilities.

Immediately we put Desmond in the utility room Jemima got up and began to quack quietly to him. He was equally responsive, and in a short time they were both eating and drinking again. The only drink available was the antibiotic solution. This meant that Jemima was only going to get half her medication and Desmond the other half. Since I could think of no way to train Desmond to have his own dish of water, I explained the problem to my vet who prescribed a second course of antibiotics to guarantee that Jemima had the whole course. After medication and about a week later, with Jemima fit and well, both ducks were returned to their outdoor accommodation and were once again spending most of the day on their pond.

A few months later I went down to the chicken pen to let the ducks and chickens out to discover that Jemima had died quite unexpectedly during the night. This was such a pity after she had survived her injuries of the previous December. Again, Desmond was distraught and spent most of the day quacking sadly in the outside run. This time there was no way we could reunite him with his best friend. So plan B came into operation – to find another Silver Appleyard duck to be a new companion for Desmond.

As our friends who had originally bred Desmond and Jemima couldn't help, we had to look further afield. We bought a local newspaper and looked in the 'poultry for sale' section for Silver Appleyard ducks; there was no Google to refer to. We eventually found a female Silver Appleyard for sale about forty miles away. David and I went to collect the duck as soon as we could. Desmond was pleased with our choice of friend, Rebecca, and began to enjoy life again. If someone had told me that I would be driving forty miles to find a suitable partner for a pet duck I would never have believed them, especially as my attitude to most things is 'minimum effort for maximum return'.

Diary of a Hero

Nero the Hero arrived today
With colitis and dandruff thick.
A brand new pup, hip hooray!
But why is he so sick?

Nero the Hero met Lynton today,
Traumatic experience that,
But they got on straight away
Tormenting Miffy the cat.

Nero the Hero went out today
And discovered our bantam cock.
A quick rough and tumble (was it play?)
Gave him a mighty shock.

Nero the Hero ate socks today.
They went down, just like that:
A trip to the vet, some might say,
Then out they came, all black.

Nero the Hero is now a big pup,
The play-fights are no joke.
The cock's outgunned but won't give up;
We simply live in hope.

Nero the Hero went swimming today
In a sluggish, muddy stream.
Black is what the coat displays,
Instead of lovely cream.

Black Jake arrived at home today,
Small, fat and full of teeth.
With Nero the Hero he did play,
Much to Lynton's relief.

Nero the Hero went back today.
Damn!

By Chris Easton

Black Jake

"Would you like a black Labrador puppy? He is outside-bred, not from Guide Dogs stock, and will need to be homed the day after tomorrow. His name is Jake."

How tempting. I had never had a black dog – Lynton didn't count, he was a German Shepherd – nor had I had an outside-bred puppy before. These are puppies that have either been donated, or have been bought by those in charge of the Guide Dogs breeding programme in Warwickshire to widen the gene pool. Having this puppy would mean an overlap with the fully grown Nero for four weeks. From the dog training side of things that wasn't going to be a problem as Nero was eleven months

Lynton training Nero and Jake

old and a well-behaved dog. It could even be an advantage, as my experience with Lynton showed. The young puppy would have two older dogs, both showing him the way it should be done.

There was still one complication – the utility room was in the middle of being revamped and that was always the base camp for a puppy. I went and looked into the utility room to survey the situation and work out what I could do. It wasn't a very promising sight – the floor was ripped up and down to bare concrete, which was no good for clearing up puddles, and there were wires and pipes on show that would normally be hidden away – far too dangerous to expose a new puppy to.

I looked at the kitchen with its round table and

chairs at one end and large island bench in the middle. As long as I was in the kitchen supervising the puppy it would be fine; my main concern was that he would need somewhere safe to go at night and for the times when he was left alone. I arranged to borrow a small cage from my supervisor that Jake could be in when I had to leave him alone in the house. It would fit in the kitchen at the end of the island bench and so it really didn't take me long to say "Yes" to Jake.

Jake was seven and a half weeks old when he arrived, slightly older than the pups are usually when they start the puppy-walking process. He weighed nearly fifteen pounds, a good weight for a pup of that age, and was very solid. He settled in well with all the family, including Lynton and Miffy, and to my relief he also loved his little cage. It was a grey heavy-duty-plastic carry-cage, not an open-meshed indoor kennel. It was plenty big enough for him. He was only going to need it for two weeks at the most until the utility room was finished and he could sleep in there. But he loved his cage much more than his bed in the utility room and would choose to curl up in there whenever the opportunity arose. Eventually I had to take the cage away, as he was really far too big for it.

Jake was quick to learn and was also fun to have around. He did get a bit over-excited when visitors came, rushing to greet them, but he always settled down after a few minutes. Eating and drinking were other notable events in Jake's life. He was a sloppy drinker. His jaw wasn't the standard V-shape, but seemed to widen out at the start of his double teeth. When he was thirsty I'm sure he only drank half the water he lapped up. The remainder came out halfway along his mouth and landed all over the floor. His water bowl was almost permanently surrounded by its own miniature lake of slobbered water. Jake also enjoyed his food… well, he was a Labrador. He ate his dinner quickly, licked the bowl spotlessly clean, inside and out, and frequently turned the bowl upside down to check the base of it. A regular question from me to the family was, "Has anyone seen Jake's bowl?" On one occasion the reply came, "No, but wherever it is it'll be upside down!" So true.

A few weeks before Jake left us I went into Reading on the train with him and David, train journeys being part of a pup's education. The three of us walked from Reading station past the parked buses, along the crowded pavements and up the main street to WH Smith's, where I left David in the audio department. I was finding it very crowded, but I don't think Jake had realised how busy it was that day. I wanted to go to Marks and Spencer's and so set off with Jake to do my own thing.

After about twenty minutes, I had finished my shopping and was going back to meet up with

David. I always talk to my dogs, giving them a running commentary on what we are doing, as it keeps them listening to me, so as we set off on the return journey I said to Jake, "Come on, let's find David." We retraced our steps through the bustle of town in a fairly purposeful manner. Just before the main entrance doors to WH Smith's I was surprised as Jake started to turn right in front of me. I was going to stop him, but then I realised that he was heading for the single side door by which we had left the shop. I was now very interested to see what he would do. I decided to let him use his initiative and just encouraged him again to find David. He went through the shop, avoiding all obstacles on the way, and took me straight to him – a natural guide dog. At that moment I was a very proud puppy-walker and job satisfaction was just about as high as it could be.

Empty yoghurt pots make good short-term toys for puppies. They shoot across the room when trodden on with a paw and they make a good crunchy noise when bitten. Jake in particular loved playing with them and we loved watching him do it. As a farewell present for Jake we decided that, as yoghurt pots were his favourite, we would make it a real treat by giving him a full yoghurt pot, rather than the usual empty one. I took a long time choosing the flavour and eventually went for raspberry, for no particular reason. I mentioned the problem I had

had deciding on a flavour, to which David replied: "We should have got blackcurrant; after all, he is black." Why didn't I think of that?

We had our lunch that day sitting around the plastic patio table in the garden enjoying the sunshine. After we had finished eating I called Jake over to give him his own complete yoghurt. I don't know what I had expected, but there was anticipation of how much he would enjoy it; after all, no other dog had been given such a treat. Jake took the pot from my hand, wolfed down the contents, crunched the pot and walked away with no sign of gratitude at all. Obviously an empty yoghurt pot was just as exciting, if not better, as a full one. The next day was a sad one as Jake left us to train as a guide dog. As I gave him his farewell pat I told him that he could come back if he needed a career change, but there was little chance of that. If he couldn't make it as a guide, then who could?

Jake was nearly two years old when he qualified. He would have qualified earlier but while in kennels he caught kennel cough, which affected his throat so badly that he had to be rested for two to three months. When he had recovered and finished his training, Jake was placed with a blind owner who lived on the outskirts of London but worked in the centre of the city. He commuted to work by train and underground every day, a challenge that Jake took in his stride.

We didn't lose contact with Jake, as his owner, Alastair, phoned us soon after he qualified to say how pleased he was with his new dog.

A working day in a guide dog's life

What follows is a day in the life of Jake the Guide Dog – from his perspective but written by his owner Alastair. It chronicles an average working day for him and his owner travelling from Harrow in North London to the City for a day's work in the financial centre of the UK and gives a real perspective on the impressive set of skills that Jake had learnt to become a guide dog.

'Jake's Day'

Whilst it is *de rigueur* to anthropomorphise dogs, if you had witnessed his very deliberate actions whilst working as a guide dog, and seen the raw intelligence in his eyes, you might have begun to believe that the canine equivalent of this imagining was a reality.

Yawn... stretch... up... shake – "That's me awake."

I wander over and prod Dad with my nose, and he fondles my ears and says, "Morning, mate; breakfast in a minute."

He disappears for a time into the little room – reassuringly normal noises of water running – and he comes back and gets dressed.

I watch carefully – "Ah, it's a suit and tie; those clothes mean today we're off to that big building with lots of people; it's not one of those rest days when Dad puts on his casual clothes."

He gives me my breakfast, the usual bowl of kibble, and after a while he strides purposefully to the front door.

"Come on, mate, let's go," he says; but I'm already there waiting, and willingly thrust my head into the white, leather harness and we leave the house.

As we leave the front garden, Dad points left, and I know for sure that we're doing the usual journey.

The neighbour has parked his car on the pavement again, so I carefully edge round it, making sure Dad doesn't hit anything; he knows, though, and gives me encouragement. This makes me happy as I love it when he understands what I'm doing and tells me so.

I snort with contentment, and we proceed to the local train station.

I am absolutely sure where we're going now, so I set about taking Dad the usual way. We have a sort of conversation as we walk along: Dad says the odd word of encouragement whilst I snort and wag my tail in appreciation.

Nothing particularly challenging today, just the usual number of people not looking where they are going, too busy talking on those funny things they hold up to their heads. Oh wait, a low branch, so I hesitate, and we edge round it.

The last stretch of road is always fun. I get to really stride out, weaving in and out of people who walk far too slowly if you ask me, picking my moments to overtake, dodging lampposts and so on.

It's really good fun as I know Dad appreciates it, and he enjoys it too. He talks to me all the time, letting me know I'm doing well, and that's all I want to do.

We enter the train station and I head for the big gate that we always use – oh, someone is in the way, but if I just go around here we can squeeze behind them and still get to the gate… Yep, there we go.

I take him to the normal staircase – we don't use the escalator in case my paws get caught in the cracks – and down we go – there's a train. "Let's hurry," says Dad.

We get on – the usual assault of smells, and ranks of sad-looking people; I wish they would cheer up and stop hiding behind those bits of paper.

I know Dad likes to go to one of those things they sit on, and I spot an empty one and show it to Dad.

We settle down and he plays with my ears again.

I am a black dog, which makes me more difficult to see, so I tuck my tail and paws in as best I can. None of the other travellers notice me and quite often stand on me, but Dad positions his feet around me, so I feel more safe.

After a long and boring journey, I recognise the bumps in the track just before we usually get off. I look up at Dad and, sure enough, he's stretching and getting ready to stand up and leave the train.

This bit is always tricky; I don't understand why everyone pushes to get on the train whilst others are trying to get off – it really doesn't make sense. Dad never asks me to guide him off the train because I couldn't do it without bumping him into people, so I just trot along beside him and we leave the train as best we can.

Now for the staircase up from the platform. This bit is fairly easy, most people are heading in the same direction, and I manage to slot in and walk with everyone else to the bottom of the stairs.

Dad clicks his tongue, which means 'on you go', and we start to mount the stairs.

Here's another thing – Dad always tries to get me to the left-hand side of the steps, and most other people seem to do the same thing, but why oh why is there always someone who thinks it's OK to try to hurry down the stairs against the flow and on the wrong side – sometimes, I just don't understand why humans try to make everything so difficult.

Dad exchanges a word with the man near the gate out of the station; he always says 'good morning' to Dad and I give him a friendly look and a wag... Why not? Everyone else looks miserable, but he is always friendly.

From here, it's an easy walk along to that big building. I take Dad to the door, through to the little metal gates we have to go through and round the corner to these weird doors in the wall.

People seem to gather around them and flow in as they open; only funny thing is, you enter a little room which just goes up or down, then you get out of the same door you got in. Very strange things these humans do, but you still end up in a difference place. Dad seems to expect it, though, so I'm not worried.

Another routine now: Dad goes to his table, puts his briefcase down then goes for coffee. He always seems to have a chat with a few people there, and some give me a kind look.

And so begins another day. The occasional trip to other rooms, lots of talking to people and only lunchtime really breaks up the day. To be honest, I spend much of the day dozing, with the occasional scratch on the head from Dad.

It's funny, sometimes when Dad is in one of those smaller rooms, you know where a few people sit round a table and just talk constantly, they all laugh at me – don't know why. I suppose it might have something to do with my stretches – I just can't help making that sort of grunting, groaning snort of satisfaction as I stretch, and they all find it funny – cheek.

No big dramas today. Sometimes a loud thing, I think they call it an alarm, goes off and everyone makes for the stairs and stands around outside for ages, in the rain sometimes, and then they all go back in again – what is the point? But everyone seems okay about it, so no big deal.

Not like that day just after we got to work, when there was a loud bang and everyone seemed really worried. That was very strange; everyone left the building that day as well, in fact everyone seemed to leave all the buildings, and there were loud cars and helicopters everywhere. That wasn't a very nice day; people were scared, and it took Dad and me ages to get home.

It turned out Dad's office is in the building right above Aldgate tube station where one of four bombs were detonated that day. It resulted in the deaths of seven people aboard that train. 8.50am on 7th July 2005.

Guide dogs need to be able to cope in all situations. This is not an experience that most people, let alone a guide dog, would encounter in their everyday life. I'm impressed with the way Jake reacted to the situation – or rather didn't react, but went about guiding his mate Al home in a calm manner despite the panic and chaos that must have surrounded him that day. Knowing Jake to be a confident and level-headed dog, he was probably revelling in an additional challenge to his everyday routine. I think he deserved a medal for his efforts, but he was probably quite happy to have his game of tug with a rope-ball, followed by his dinner, when he eventually got home.

Lunchtimes are good – we go to various places, and Dad often meets up with others and we go somewhere for a sit-down where there are carpets to lie on – I like those. But not today; it's a quick trip to the sandwich shop and back to his table.

I can always tell when it's nearly time to go home – the atmosphere changes and people start putting things away, gathering up jackets, umbrellas and other items, and talking more cheerfully to each other.

Sure enough, before long, Dad stretches and says, "Come on, mate, time to head home."

And we do the journey in reverse.

Today's journey home is much like any other, and today seems to be one of those days when Dad pops into the shop on the way home – oh yes, one interesting thing that happened was that we were just nearing home when a car pulled out of a driveway really fast. Silly, really – there are tall hedges in the way, so whoever is driving can't possibly see if anyone is coming along the pavement, so I don't understand why they do it so fast. I see it coming, though, and stop dead.

Dad is really pleased with this one; he crouches down and gives me a hug and an ear-rub all at the same time – I mean, I know he's pleased and I've stopped the car hitting him, but I didn't much fancy being run over either.

We reach the house, and I head straight for the water bowl. Dad notices and fills it up with nice fresh, cold water.

After this, Dad always changes his clothes having already put the kettle on – he always does the same things when we get home.

I retire to my cushion for a while and watch Dad put the radio on and drink his cup of tea.

I get up hopefully, collect a rope from the toy box and take it over; yep, Dad grabs the end and we have a tug of war for a while. This involves lots of tugging around the floor, getting my ears rubbed and jumping up to catch the dangling end. Then I go to get a ball, which I love to catch, and we play with that for a while. We often do this in the garden, but it's started raining so we don't go out there today.

The rest of the evening is nice and familiar; Dad plays his guitar for a while (what a racket!) and we both have some dinner.

Eventually, Dad takes me outside for the last time before we both go to sleep for the night.

"Good night, mate," says Dad, giving me a last pat, and I settle down, wondering whether it's another office day tomorrow, or maybe it'll be one of those lazy days. Even better, it might be one of those days where we go somewhere new; I always enjoy those.

Pity Dad can't tell me, but it would spoil the surprise.

Stretch, snuggle, curl up – yawn, snore – good night!

Animal rescue

On the first Saturday morning after David's fourteenth birthday, he went to work as a volunteer at the Wokingham Animal Rescue Centre. We had agreed to him helping there on one condition – that he didn't bring anything home. Well, you can always hope.

The Animal Rescue Centre was a huddle of mismatched buildings that were situated on the edge of farmland on the outskirts of Wokingham and could be reached by going down a gravel track. It was too far for David to cycle, so we had to drive him there for his 9am start that first morning. He really enjoyed himself, we hadn't expected anything else to be honest, and after a few weeks we would drop him off in the morning and he would happily spend all day there on a Saturday. The work included cleaning hutches, cages and kennels, and feeding the animals.

The bonus of the job was building up a rapport with the animals. His first favourite was a male polecat ferret called Gordon, nicknamed 'Gordon What-a-Mess'. I could always tell when he had been handling Gordon a lot during the day as there was a very distinct, not-too-pleasant aroma in my car on the journey home after his day at the rescue centre. Thank goodness for soap and showers.

It wasn't long before the question, "Could we give Gordon a good home?" was put to me by David. I know I'm a soft touch when it comes to animals, but I wasn't too sure about having a polecat. I had seen Gordon and handled him and, although he was very tame, I wasn't impressed with the smell, even though he would be living in the garden, not in the house. I stuck to my guns and said, "No," so Gordon stayed at the rescue centre and was eventually rehomed. It was a very sad teenager that I collected from animal rescue that Saturday. I felt a bit mean at this stage, as David had built up a good rapport with the animal and was very fond of him. In a moment of weakness, I had said that he could have the next tame female polecat that was brought into the centre. Females don't smell as strongly as the males.

A couple of months later, two female polecats were brought into the Animal Rescue Centre to be rehomed, but that was the one Saturday that David was ill and couldn't go to work. Two other helpers who were there on the day were allowed to adopt them. David was very disappointed as we were still polecat free.

Just before Christmas that year, three guinea pigs were brought to the centre – a mother with two babies, a male and a female. "Can I have the two females, Mum?" asked Dave. Chris has a soft spot for guinea pigs and was keen on having them, so we said, "Yes." The following Saturday all three animals arrived home with David. "Can we look after the male too until there is a suitable rabbit for him to share a hutch with?" Harry, as he became known, didn't go back to the rescue centre. Julie fancied keeping him, so David made a hutch and gave it and the guinea pig to Julie for her Christmas present. We kept the H theme for the females' names and called them Henrietta and Hattie. Henrietta was the mother. She was tri-coloured and long-haired. Hattie was black and tan, and Harry was all black, but they were both short-haired.

We handled the animals most days, partly for fun but also to make sure they were tame. There is little or no pleasure in having an aggressive pet. As the weeks went by we could see that Hattie and Harry were growing. I also had the feeling that

Henrietta was getting larger, and was beginning to get suspicious as to why.

Sure enough, one Saturday when David came back from Animal Rescue, he went to look at his two guinea pigs but found there were now four in the hutch. Henrietta had had two babies. One was white with a black head, the other was all black. This was when we discovered that baby guinea pigs are very, very cute. The two babies looked just the same as an adult guinea pig, but in miniature, being about the size of a hamster. They were both females and would be able to stay with Henrietta and Hattie, but more accommodation was needed. Instead of building another hutch, David built an extension to the existing one.

Since we had had a sneaking feeling that Henrietta was pregnant we had already begun to think of suitable names for any babies. At the time, Mark was looking for a job in civil engineering. Kier and Costain were two of the companies he was interested in, so we called the black guinea pig Costain and the predominantly white one Kier.

During the winter, all the guinea pigs were kept in their hutches under our covered sideway, where they were warmer than they would have been if they were in the garden. At night we would cover the mesh part of the front of the hutches with thick blankets. As soon as it was warm enough for them to be outside, the hutches were put on the lawn and we attached enclosed chicken wire runs to them so that the guinea pigs could stretch their legs and have fresh grass to eat. Some days we even let them run free in the garden, and either Harry or the four females would be let out.

One day, when it was Harry's turn to run free, David and I went into the front garden to cut the hedge. After a while we became aware that Lynton, out in the back garden, was barking. Not continual barking, but single barks with about a five-second interval between each one. This was quite unusual so, after about ten minutes of this, we went to investigate his problem.

We found Lynton trying to shepherd Harry back into his hutch, but Harry wasn't co-operating. Normally, Lynton was quite happy with the guinea pigs running free, but as we were not there he felt that he was responsible for Harry's wellbeing and wanted him safely behind bars. Harry was about two yards from his open hutch but backing it. He still felt he needed to free run. Lynton was about another two yards away, facing Harry and still trying to get him to go home. They had reached stalemate. I picked up Harry and examined him. He had a wound on the back of his neck. It looked as if Lynton had tried to pick Harry up and put him back into the hutch where he felt he should be. At this point Lynton decided he was 'off duty'. He left us in charge of Harry and went off to do his own thing.

Considering the difference in size between the two animals, it would have been easy for Lynton to kill Harry with one bite. The fact that Harry was still alive showed that Lynton's actions were well-intentioned and that Harry's safety was paramount in his mind. However, the guinea pig's injury required a trip to the vet. More worryingly, how were we going to explain this to Julie? All's well that ends well and, after a short period of convalescence in the utility room, Harry returned to roam the garden again, but never again under the sole charge of the shepherding dog.

Enter polecats

Now we had five guinea pigs but, to my relief and David's disappointment, still no polecats. David was going to have to wait a little longer. It wasn't until about four months after the guinea pigs came to live with us that two more tame polecats were brought into Animal Rescue, much to David's delight. We said he could have the female, and on the Monday evening after school we went to collect Lucy. She was a good-looking, dark brown polecat with a white throat. We brought her home and put her in a large hutch under our covered sideway. She wasn't very impressed with the way we had arranged it and, as soon as she had sniffed around her new quarters, she very busily moved all the bedding around. She was much livelier than Gordon, and I was beginning to have second thoughts about having a polecat for a pet if I was going to have to handle her a lot.

That evening, while David was upstairs doing his homework, I decided to have a go at bonding with Lucy – I needed to be able to confidently handle any of the pets that we had, and now seemed to be as good a time as any to get to know her. I picked up Lucy quite confidently and started handling her, but it wasn't long before she bit me. I put her back into the cage, feeling a little disheartened. She was going to be David's pet, and I had developed a soft spot for the animals, but not for one that was going to bite. I went to tell David what had happened. He came downstairs to see Lucy and picked her up. David is good at handling all animals, so he was a bit taken aback when Lucy bit him. I made the decision there and then that Lucy would have to return to Animal Rescue and we would have the next tame female that was brought in. We were both a little despondent as we returned to the house and cleaned the bites she had given us.

We couldn't take her back Tuesday evening because David was playing cricket after school, and so Wednesday evening was the first convenient time to return her, but in the end that didn't happen. On Wednesday morning, David went outside to feed Lucy, but it wasn't long before he returned to the house with an unusual observation...

"Mum, the hay is squeaking." I left my half-eaten bowl of cereal and rushed out with him to have a look. On close inspection of the bedding we could see eight babies, each one barely an inch long, pink and eyes closed. No wonder Lucy wasn't very happy when we were picking her up, if she was about to give birth.

Now plan B came into operation. Instead of taking Lucy back to Animal Rescue we decided to keep her and her eight babies until they were six weeks old, then take everyone back to be rehomed. We had never looked after one adult polecat so we were really challenged with eight babies as well. We started by feeding Lucy cooked chicken – the babies only needed her milk at this stage. We checked the eight babies every day and handled them fairly frequently. They were in the sleeping quarters where we had put hay for their bedding, and we had to be very careful that they didn't fall out when we opened the door.

After about two weeks, with the babies growing well on their mother's milk, we were beginning to think they would soon be going onto solid food, so we sought advice from a polecat expert on rearing the animals. We were told to give Lucy raw food, such as chicken, minced beef or fish, and a vitamin supplement. The babies would eventually need brown bread soaked in milk. It was also important not to disturb the babies for the first couple of weeks. We had been doing everything wrong but, despite that, our family was thriving. Lucy tried the bread and milk but wasn't impressed with it. We gave her the tip of a raw chicken wing, which was much more to her liking. So much so that she took it out of her bowl and hid it in her larder at the back of the sleeping quarters. Not wanting to infect her quarters with rotting meat, after that we gave her small pieces of chicken first of all and then a bone to gnaw at as an 'after dinner' treat.

Lucy always went to the toilet in the same part of the hutch – in the far end of the open area – so when we realised this we put a litter tray in that corner. She liked her litter tray, went to the toilet at one end of it and, in the daytime, relaxed at the other end. For the first three weeks, the babies went to the toilet in the corners of the sleeping area. The hutch needed regular cleaning to keep it hygienic and smelling respectable. Disinfectant and clean newspaper was my solution to the problem, but Lucy had other ideas. She kept sniffing the walls and floors – disinfectant wasn't her favourite perfume – and then she completely rearranged the clean sheets of newspaper that I had put in the hutch, scrabbling them into torn pieces and completely ruining my nice, neat presentation.

After about three weeks the babies began to venture out of the nest into the open area. At this age they still had their eyes closed. Lucy must have felt they were too young to be that adventurous as she picked them up by the scruff of the neck and threw them back into the sleeping quarters whenever they appeared at the door. After a couple of days of trying to keep them all in the sleeping quarters she realised that she was fighting a losing battle and let them stay out with her.

As the babies became more adventurous we handled them daily to make sure they would be tame. I was still frightened of Lucy, so I only got them out for a cuddle when she was sound asleep. To make sure I handled all of them, I put each one in a bucket after it had had a cuddle. When there were eight babies in the bucket, I put them back into the hutch. We had one male and seven females. The male was the first one to leave the nest, so we called him Columbus, after Christopher Columbus the explorer. He had a beige body, dark head and mask, and four dark feet. The smallest female had similar markings and we called her Midge. Two more had dark feet, the other four had white feet, and that was as good as I ever got with my identification of them. Despite handling each baby every day, the four with the white feet were never as friendly as the ones with the dark feet. It must have been something in their genes.

At four weeks old, the first baby opened her eyes, but it was five weeks before the last baby, Columbus, opened his. It was getting easier to pick them up;

by now they each weighed between six and eight ounces and were very active. They began to lap at their milk and eat the bread and milk. Lucy's milk was drying up by now so they had to be able to feed themselves, and they soon started to eat the raw chicken. Columbus was the tamest baby and would take food from my hand. At five weeks, they were very active and would have rough-and-tumbles in the cage. It was becoming obvious that they were going to need more space, and so we attached a run to the hutch to increase the play area. In it there were pieces of wood, some pipes for them to run through, a ball and a bowl of water. Lucy would paddle in the water and then roll in a towel. David picked her up, and although she mouthed him she didn't bite. He let her walk onto his hand and up his arm and she was fine, but I still wasn't brave enough to hold her. Lucy liked the milk we gave her but her very favourite treat was a quail's egg.

By six weeks, the babies were fully weaned and in a fairly set routine of eating, sleeping and playing. I fed them three times a day, at 8am, 1pm and 6pm, with a snack at bedtime. I gave them their meat first and then their bread and milk. They all ate vigorously, especially the four white-footed females. Keeping the hutch clean became a full-time job. The bedding and litter tray had to be changed daily. I couldn't do it as well as I would have liked because of Lucy, not because I was afraid of her biting me but more out of

The polecats at four weeks old

concern that she would escape. At the time I didn't know how to catch a free running polecat, although I have since learnt that if you squeak a toy, they think it is a baby and come running.

At six and a half weeks it was time to return the polecats to the Animal Rescue Centre to be rehomed, but in the end only Lucy and six babies went back. We had tamed our own polecats and decided to keep our two favourites, Columbus and Midge; so much for not having a male polecat because of their strong aroma. Looking after Lucy and her eight babies had been unexpected and fun. In spite of my initial doubts, it had been a great experience, which I wouldn't have wanted to miss, even if they were big time-wasters.

Rudge, Gazza, Rebel and the return of Errol

O ne Monday morning, soon after Jake had left us, I phoned the Guide Dogs Centre to speak to my supervisor, Debi. "Ah, we've been talking about you," she said. "We wondered if you would like to walk a chocolate Labrador? There is an outside-bred one which has been bought by the association and is due to be placed on Wednesday." Of course, I couldn't refuse such a request. Chocolate Labrador guide dog puppies are not very common, and I had read and enjoyed the book *Emma and I*, the story of a guide dog owner and her chocolate Labrador. Her guide dog, Emma, stole

Rudge at ten weeks old

the hearts of all her readers, including me, and as a result the thought of walking a chocolate Labrador really appealed. Everything was arranged for the pup to be delivered on Wednesday afternoon. I decided not to tell the family and just surprise them.

David arrived home from school at the same time as the pup arrived. Seeing Debi's car, he asked if it was another pup – a black Labrador was his first guess. When I said, "No," he replied with, "Oh, not another yellow one," which just showed how we had all been a little scarred by our recent experiences of yellow Labrador puppies. He couldn't guess, but his enthusiasm was reignited when I told him that it was a chocolate Labrador named Rudge.

Getting to know your pup is an exciting part of the job. Just like children, they gradually reveal parts of their character as they meet new experiences, and it's not long before I am finding similarities with other dogs, recognising favourable habits and identifying individual quirks, skills and talents in each pup. Rudge passed the number one test with flying colours – he was good in the house, not too lively or destructive. On the skills and talents side, Rudge soon started to show a real interest in the dog toys, showing natural skills as he worked out what he could do with each one. Rudge's favourite toy was a frisbee and he soon perfected the art of picking it up off the floor when it was rim side down. He put his right paw over the top of the toy and pulled it towards him onto the top of his left paw. With part of the rim off the floor, he could then pick it up with his mouth – simple. Playing with toys was definitely a good way to get this pup to use his grey cells.

Rudge soon met all our pets: chickens, tortoises, guinea pigs, Miffy the cat, Lynton the dog, plus Midge and Columbus our two polecats. He got on well with them all – well, with most of them. His big mistake was to investigate the polecats at close quarters. His intentions were totally innocent as he poked his nose against the edge of the cage to wash the polecat's nose. Midge was not taking any chances with a dog checking out her home. I was in the kitchen when I suddenly heard Rudge crying quite loudly. I looked out of the window to see what was happening and saw Midge biting Rudge's tongue through the wire netting with him backing away as fast as he could. Between the two of them Rudge's tongue was gradually stretching out further and further just like an elastic band. I left the kitchen, heading for the polecat cage as fast as I could. It must have been at least ten seconds before I reached them, at which point Midge let go. This was a good job really, as I wasn't quite sure how I was going to release her grip on his tongue, nor did I realise that a Labrador puppy had such a long tongue. Rudge learnt from this ten-second experience never to go anywhere near a polecat. With their cage being situated on the patio to the left-hand side of the garden path, Rudge now kept to the right-hand side close to the garage wall, while glancing left to make sure that Midge, who was in her cage at least a metre away, could not subject him to tongue torture again. So, the saying 'once bitten, twice shy' turned out to be true in this case.

If being good in the house was a strong point with Rudge, then road-walking was the opposite. Although happy to walk out of the house and garden and unafraid of traffic, he was reluctant to walk along the centre of the pavement. When on my left-hand side and next to the road, he kept to the outside edge of the pavement and walked along the kerb stones – not the safest place to be if he slipped. He also found it difficult to concentrate on the job in hand and, after a few minutes of walking, he would get distracted and start to sniff the air, evidence of his gun dog breeding. He didn't have much stamina either. This was not unusual for a young puppy, but even at nine months old he could only manage a twenty-minute walk. We joked that he would need a guide dog owner who didn't want to go any further than the corner shop and back, but I wasn't sure there were many who would fit that bill.

Six months before Rudge arrived, Lynton had been diagnosed with kidney failure and this, together with his pancreatic deficiency and eventual muscle degeneration in his hind legs, made him a very sick dog. Rudge was a gentle and sensitive puppy, which was the ideal temperament to have in the house with our very sick older dog. Despite his health problems, Lynton still enjoyed his daily walks and, although losing weight, he never looked sick. He was happy sharing his home with Rudge, who hadn't needed the disciplining that Lynton had felt necessary for some of our other pups, and the two of them developed a good bond. Rudge was seven months old when Lynton rapidly went downhill over a twenty-four hour period and we had to make the decision to have him put to sleep – a very sad day. Rudge was now an only dog, but not for long.

A couple of weeks after Lynton died, I paid a visit to Folly Court, Wokingham Guide Dogs Centre, to return some of his medication. While I was waiting

I had a chat to the receptionist who quite casually asked if I would like to have Gazza. I was beginning to think I might have been getting a reputation for being a bit of a soft touch. "Who's Gazza?" I asked.

Gazza turned out to be a thirteen-and-a-half-year-old retired black Labrador guide dog. His owner could no longer keep him as Gazza was becoming bowel incontinent and was currently living in the kennel block at Wokingham. Everyone thought it a shame that such an elderly dog was living in kennels. I didn't really want to take on another dog but, not wanting to turn him down without proper consideration, I asked if I could see him. That's when Gary, nicknamed Gazza, was brought to see me – or me to see him, really, as it soon became obvious that incontinence wasn't his only problem. As he stood there, gazing at me with cloudy, cataract-filled eyes, his mouth was open in an enormous smile and he wagged his tail very happily in a circular motion. Despite his problems he won me over with that big smile on his face. He knew a soft touch when he met one.

I agreed to take him home with me and board him until the staff could rehome him. Gazza happily got into my car and home we went to break the news to the family. I didn't have to say much because Gazza walked into the house and met the family with the same happy smile and waggy tail that had attracted me to him just an hour before.

Next, he introduced himself to Rudge by picking up a squeaky toy and challenging him to a game. Rudge wasn't sure what to do. My house rule was 'No playing in the lounge', but Gazza didn't know this. Rudge didn't know what to do at first, as he knew it was against the rules, but it was very tempting. He eventually gave in and took up the challenge. Things were a bit riotous and so I called Gazza several times to stop him playing, but with no success. Eventually I told Rudge to stop, which he did, straight away. It was at this stage that I realised that not only was Gazza's sight very poor, but he couldn't hear either. It was probably a good job I was only boarding him.

A couple of months after Gazza arrived I had to go into hospital for major surgery, which meant the rest of the family were on dog duty for a while. The family could cope with looking after Gazza, but Rudge's needs were more demanding, and so he left us and went to live with my supervisor, Debi, for a month, before going into kennels at ten months old. I think by this time we had all realised that Gazza was not going to be rehomed and we had happily accepted him into the family for the foreseeable future.

After being without a puppy for only a few weeks, and with me back home and on the mend, we were all getting withdrawal symptoms, so I put in a request for another pup. I was offered another black Labrador called Rebel who, it subsequently turned out, was related to Gazza – he was his nephew, so it would be interesting to see if Rebel had any similar traits to his uncle. Rebel was another easy pup to train – fairly laid back and not fazed by anything. If anything, he was a bit aloof. I hadn't known Gazza as a pup but, from the way he was living life to the full, in spite of all his problems, I had the feeling that he would have been much more of a challenge to walk than Rebel.

So now we had two dogs again and our family seemed quite balanced. A few weeks later, though, all that changed. Out of the blue we had a phone call asking, "Do you want a dog?" I recognised the voice of Arthur, Errol's owner, who had kept in touch with us and periodically phoned me to relate Errol's latest escapades, always opening the phone call with, "Do you want a dog?" This time I had a feeling that he was serious. Errol was eleven and a half years old and was due to retire, having had a good career and been an excellent working guide dog. Although he was still working well, I knew he had had a fatty tumour removed from his chest and his harness would be rubbing on that area. Errol's owner lived in a small house, so living with a new guide dog and Errol would be difficult. So it was a serious question and he did want us to have Errol when he retired. It didn't take us long to say "Yes". We had always had a soft spot in our hearts for that dog, despite the fact that he was a bit of a rogue.

Four weeks after Rebel arrived, Errol came to rejoin the family. We went to collect him from Arthur, who lived in Kent. At the time I hadn't seen Errol for about seven years and when he came to the door with his owner he totally ignored me. I was very impressed with his impeccable behaviour, but a little disappointed with his lack of recognition. Anyway, I spoke to him and gave him a good pat and cuddle. I think at this stage his computer brain was counting back the years, and after about a minute he must have reached 1985 where I fitted into his life. At this point the calm sedate Labrador suddenly changed into a lunatic. I was glad he had eventually remembered me, and with so much enthusiasm, particularly as he was going to spend his retirement with us.

Once back home, Errol instantly slotted into our routine – or did we just adapt to his way of doing things? Within five minutes of his arrival, tea towels were moved into a crumpled heap on the kitchen work surface instead of on the towel rail, otherwise Errol would take them and drag them around the kitchen floor. Food had to be put at the back of the work surfaces or in a cupboard to prevent the four-legged vacuum cleaner clearing the surfaces for us. These were puppy traits. I thought that even Errol would have grown out of them at his age – but no! I could see we were going to be kept on our toes for the next few years.

Errol the senior citizen

After Errol's arrival in September we rapidly increased our level of surveillance and by December we thought we had the better of him, but not for long. Christmas offers so many more opportunities for a dog like Errol and we were rather too preoccupied with the festive preparations to give him our undivided attention. A couple of weeks before Christmas, a friend came to visit us after shopping in Reading. While we chatted happily in the lounge, Errol made his escape from the kitchen into the hall. There he found our friend's large shopping bag on the floor. This was not a place where we would leave our bags, but our unsuspecting friend was not used to living with Errol, and we hadn't noticed. He just had to check out things and, to his delight, he found a packet of chocolate Christmas tree decorations which, of course, he had to eat. Later we discovered that the chocolates had been in the bottom of the bag, not just an easy picking at the top. Chocolate is very widely publicised as being poisonous to dogs, but thankfully it didn't seem to have any effect on Errol as his chocolate incidents were not limited to raiding shopping bags.

At Christmas, in the lounge, we always have a tree decorated with fairy lights, tinsel, baubles and chocolates. Being conscious of Errol's misdemeanours with the chocolates in the bag, I made sure that he didn't have access to the lounge and kept the appropriate doors closed. At least he couldn't open them. Inevitably, I suppose, I forgot to close one once. After a few minutes I realised what I had done and rushed into the lounge, and there was Errol having eaten all the chocolates within reach. My immediate reaction was to gasp in amazement and then say his name in a fairly firm way. His response was instant. He knew he was in the wrong and immediately turned around and ran. Unfortunately, he had tinsel and fairy lights tangled around him and, in his attempt to make a quick getaway, they and the tree came with him. After this episode we decided to abandon the idea of chocolate decorations on future Christmas trees.

Chocolate was definitely Errol's Achilles' heel, not to mention cake and bread. Our walk-in wardrobe was an ideal place to hide Christmas presents from the children and, with a stairgate, a bedroom door and a wardrobe door all closed, we thought Errol stood no chance of reaching the few chocolate treats in the carrier bag in the cupboard. Again the inevitable happened. The stairgate was left open, the two doors were ajar and the opportunist thief stole his booty from the carrier bag.

And so it continued. There are claw marks on the sideboard from when he tried to get an apple out of the fruit bowl, and more claw marks on the fire surround from when he was trying to reach a chocolate orange on the mantelpiece. Interestingly, he never stole any meat. He always kept himself focused on cake, bread, chocolate and apples. Errol, like most Labradors, was ruled by his appetite.

Errol; nothing lasts forever

A neighbour, who lived three doors away, rang me one morning saying, "Have you lost Errol?" "No," I replied. "Well, let me put it another way. He is in my kitchen and has just eaten the cat's food." It was a good job the neighbour was an animal lover and was more concerned that Errol was away from home than the fact that he had eaten their cat's food.

Errol must have made a mental note of the easy pickings from this house because at his next opportunity he set off in that direction. We had returned from a New Year's Eve party at about 1am.

Errol and Rudge came to greet us and then we went to see Rebel. After a few minutes, we realised that Errol was missing, and we knew he would be up to no good. He must have slipped out of the front door before we had closed it. Guessing that he would have headed towards the neighbour's house again, we went in that direction to find him. Normally I would have called and whistled Errol to get him back, but as that was not very neighbour-friendly behaviour for the middle of the night I was limited to calling him in a whisper, which was a fairly futile exercise. It was a good job he was a very pale yellow Labrador and showed up reasonably well in the street lighting. As expected, we found him in the neighbour's garden looking for another treat.

Errol was generally a fit dog, but when he was about fourteen years old he had to have an operation to remove a tooth, which was the reason for his smelly breath. When he had this operation the vet discovered a tumour in his throat, so he had to have it removed the following week. He was due to stay in the Guide Dogs kennels for a few days while he recuperated, but Errol had other ideas. He never liked doors being closed on him, even if he didn't want to go anywhere, so he protested about being in a hospital kennel – Errol style. Although he could see everything that was going on, his method of complaining was to bark continually. Eventually, the kennel staff gave in and phoned me after forty-eight hours to come and collect him because he was disturbing the peace, and all that barking wasn't going to be conducive to a good recovery. Once he was back home the barking stopped and Errol was fine – once more he had got his own way.

Despite having had an operation on his throat, Errol seemed oblivious to the fact that he was supposed to be recuperating and was still happy to help himself to any food that he fancied off the table. We had friends staying for the weekend and I had made a blackcurrant crumble with the few fruits I had picked off our bush. This was a real treat as that particular fruit bush only produced a limited crop, just enough for one crumble per season. Errol obviously felt that he deserved the best and that that treat was just for him. When I went into the dining room, I wondered why there were bits of crumble on Chris's plate. Then I saw that there was some crumble missing from the main dish. Although we had three dogs to choose from, I knew at once who the culprit would be. I kept calm, took Errol by the collar and put him in the utility room. He didn't complain about being shut in there, so I knew he had a guilty conscience. Our friends felt sorry for him and said it was probably Rudge, the younger dog, who had stolen the food. Surely, as an old dog, Errol wouldn't have done the deed? After about half an hour I relented and decided to let Errol join us again. It then became obvious to all of us that he was definitely the pudding thief as the left side of his face gave him away – it was covered in blackcurrant juice and crumble.

Errol soldiered on for another year, but then one morning he had a stroke. As I was getting the dogs' breakfasts ready, Rudge and the puppy were sitting next to me, but Errol remained lying down on the kitchen floor, barking. He couldn't get up to get his dinner and was barking in frustration, so I took his dinner to him. He ate it with enthusiasm, but couldn't move himself around at all. His front end was still working, but his back end wasn't, and he couldn't live like that. Sadly, I called the vet, who came at lunchtime to put him to sleep. Our house was a much quieter and emptier place without Errol's larger-than-life character.

We buried him in the garden the next day. As he traditionally always had the last piece of toast after breakfast, I decided to be a bit sentimental and went and got the last piece of toast to put in the grave with him. Rudge brought even more tears to our eyes by going and getting Errol's blanket and dropping it in the bottom of the hole and then looking at us, as if to say, 'He'll need that, won't he?'

Errol Isn't Here

For three and a half years we had three dogs about the house: Gazza, Errol and Rebel. When a puppy goes to the vet to be neutered (all puppies are neutered before they become working guide dogs), life is much quieter at home; all puppy-walkers will know what I mean. So when Errol, the retired guide dog, went in for an operation to remove a tumour in his throat, I was inspired to write this poem.

We haven't put the stairgate up,
It does seem very queer,
But there's no need to use it
     Because Errol isn't here.

We can have the front door open,
Talk to friends from far and near,
Life is much more civilised –
     Because Errol isn't here.

I can let Rudge in the garden,
And let him wander there,
Because he doesn't misbehave,
     When Errol isn't here.

The bread is on the bread board
And no one has to fear
That it won't be there at tea time
　　　Because Errol isn't here.

We can leave the fruit and chocolates
On the table or the chair.
They will still be there for later
　　　Because Errol isn't here.

I had a call from Guide Dogs
Who said "I know he is a dear,
But he just won't stop barking.
　　　He doesn't like it here."

I rushed to bring him home again
And gave a great big cheer.
It's great that he is better;
　　　We do want Errol here!

By Monica Easton

This poem is a brief story of Errol's life; he was a superb guide, but a loveable rogue when off duty.

When Errol came to live with us
He was nearly ten weeks old.
His first-time walkers couldn't cope
Was the story we were told.

"He chews the chairs, the children's shoes
And he tiddles on the floor."
Every puppy will do this,
BUT... Errol did it more!

He chewed our hats, gloves, socks and shoes,
Mark's favourite shirt was shredded,
Towels, blankets, cuddly toys...
We'll have that pup beheaded!

Stealing food – another trait,
Which got him into trouble.
Bread, toast, cakes and chocolate:
He'd eat them at the double.

At five months old he rose to fame
And featured in a book.
Guide Dog is the name of it,
If you want to have a look.

His social habits were quite bad,
But working he was great.
He whistled through his training
And in Surrey he was placed.

His owner found him very strong
And so they had to part.
Next time he trained with Arthur
And made a brand new start.

Errol now had found his match
And both worked well together.
A sense of humour they both had
And lived 'Happy Errol Arthur'.

At eleven years retirement came,
To Errol, not to Arthur.
We were asked to have him back
And educate him further.

He didn't realise his age
And walked for miles each day,
He still stole food like toast and cake,
Would he ever mend his ways?

At fourteen years he had an op
For a tumour in his throat.
He soldiered on another year,
But then he had a stroke.

He lay still on the kitchen floor,
But food still dominated.
He whined, barked and protested
'Til breakfast was presented.

He ate some toast, but didn't move,
He stayed there all the morning.
The time had come to call the vet.
You know why he was calling.

The end had come, we had to part,
There were lumps in all our throats.
He'd made an impact on all our lives,
That loveable, cheeky rogue!

By Monica Easton

Rudge returns

J ust before Christmas, during the coffee and mince pie social morning at the Wokingham Guide Dogs Centre, there was usually a chance for puppy-walkers to talk to their puppy's trainer and find out how he or she was getting on; a doggy version of a parents' evening at school. At this time Rudge had been in kennels for about five months and was on advanced training when I had my first chance to chat to his trainer. He got a good report in lots of areas but, reading between the lines, it sounded as if there were a couple of problems that would have to be solved before Rudge could qualify as a guide dog. He showed lack of concentration and had begun showing some stress-related behaviours.

When I was walking him as a puppy I had noted his lack of concentration, so this did not come as a surprise but, as far as I was concerned, stress-related behaviours had never been an issue. It would depend on how these two areas developed as to whether Rudge would qualify as a guide dog. It wasn't long before the decision was made, and it turned out that he couldn't cope with the extra responsibility required of him to be a guide dog.

In the middle of January, I had a phone call to say that Rudge needed a career change, offering him back to me as a pet. This was a difficult decision as he wasn't one of my favourite dogs, although there was a part of me that did have a bit of a soft spot for him. Since we already had three dogs in the house, the two retired dogs, Gazza and Errol, plus the puppy Rebel, the house was feeling rather full and the rest of the family weren't sure we would cope with four dogs around, so I decided not to have him back. As I returned Guide Dogs' call I did wonder what the future would hold for him, knowing he was a sensitive dog. I felt I was letting him down as he had trusted me completely as a puppy and I was sending him off into the unknown. Rudge would now be offered to another charity, Dogs for the Disabled (now Dogs for Good) to see if he had the attributes that they needed in a dog. Before he went to them I asked if I could come and see him to give him a farewell pat and cuddle before he went out of my life forever.

I went to see him in kennels the next day and waited in a small room, which had a chair, a table, a sink unit and a few dog toys, while a member of staff went off to get him. I don't know what I had expected to happen when Rudge came in – a happy wag and a stroke maybe and then a dog confidently going off with the kennel staff. That certainly wasn't the reality. The moment Rudge saw me he went wild with excitement, jumping up at me and even jumping on the table to get closer to me, behaviour I had never seen in him before as he had always been a fairly reserved dog. I could see how the stress of the job had affected him and why the trainer decided the work was not for him. When Rudge had calmed down a bit, I went out into the free-run pen with him and we played with a ball. He was only too pleased to fetch the toy, bring it back to me and drop it. I was beginning to warm to him and was wishing I hadn't said that I didn't want him back.

I went home and talked to the family, now certain that I wanted to keep him if at all possible, and convinced them that if he didn't make it as an assistance dog for Dogs for the Disabled I would ask if I could have him back. With them in agreement I phoned the rehoming officer with this request, but she was on holiday and I had to wait a very long week before I could speak to her. When I did make contact I discovered that he wasn't wanted by Dogs for the Disabled as, at the time, they were waiting for new premises to be completed and could not accommodate him for at least two months. I could have him back.

My immediate excitement was quashed when the rehoming officer told me that she had a suitable owner on her waiting list. However, when she had tried to phone him there had been no reply and, as she had been unwilling to leave a message on his answer phone, Rudge was still available. Some things are just meant to be; so he came back to join the pack. This time I was ready for the manic behaviour when we met him from kennels. Rudge was excited to come home with me and enthusiastically greeted the two- and four-legged members of his family. I could see him starting to unwind in the company of his old friends and familiar surroundings. His shallow concentration wasn't an issue for him as a pet, and the stress-related behaviours reduced as he relaxed back into the environment where he was comfortable and the stress was removed.

23

Reliable Rudge,
the agility dog

Rudge turned out to be a very intelligent, but rather strange dog. He loved to retrieve a ball or a toy and could still pick up a frisbee when it was convex side up and on a hard surface. I could play hide-and-seek with him. He would go into the utility room when I asked him to 'hide his eyes' while I hid a toy somewhere in the house. Then he would sniff round the house and very quickly find where it had been hidden. He could also distinguish between different toys such as a kong, frame ball, etc. If I hid two toys and asked him to find a specific one, he would do so, leaving the other one still hidden. This raised the game to a higher level but, after playing it for about ten minutes, he would be mentally exhausted and have to stop.

Rudge could put his head into water and keep it there for a good ten seconds to recover a sunken toy, particularly out of the edge of our fish pond. On a few occasions on a walk he even found balls, not belonging to us, in the deepest parts of large puddles – one was ten yards in diameter and one foot deep in the middle. If he dropped a ball on a free run I could send him back to find it. He could retrace his steps at least the length of a football pitch to go to find a lost ball. This skill was put to good use when Errol was ageing and his hearing and eyesight were not as good as they used to be. On a walk, Errol would lose all sense of direction and then start to run to find me, often in the wrong direction. I could tell Rudge to fetch Errol, and he would run straight to him, nudge him on his side, then turn round and run back to me. Errol immediately turned and followed Rudge, which saved me a lot of leg power and fruitless calling of a deaf dog.

Rudge loved to carry things, especially for me. Bringing selected shopping items in from the car was one of his specialities. Not everything was suitable for him to carry, e.g. a jar of honey, a bag of fruit, etc., but I did select a few items that made him feel useful, and I could live with them being slightly worse for the experience. A pack of nine

Rudge returns, hunting for balls in puddles

toilet rolls always offered him a challenge, and it was interesting to hear the family's comments when a new roll appeared with the first few sheets being a little tatty – "I see Rudge helped unload the shopping, then."

He could manage a packet of cereal – again the cardboard box suffered a bit, but the polythene bag with the cereal inside was always intact. To help Rudge, and to protect my shopping more, I made him a drawstring shopping bag. This way I could send him off with the smaller items without fear of them being damaged. He could carry a tin of baked beans or a packet of teabags this way. I tried him with a carton of cocoa once, but his bite was a bit too enthusiastic. When I opened the shopping bag I discovered the lid had popped off and there was quite a lot of cocoa 'free running' in his bag. He did give a new dimension to my shopping list.

About a year after Rudge returned home to live with us, two puppy-walking friends of mine also had puppies that needed a career change and they had them back as pets. One was a chocolate Labrador called Rolo, who was Rudge's half-brother, and the other was a golden retriever called Nula. We decided to take them to dog agility to give them some exercise and a chance to use their brains. In dog agility they learn to negotiate a variety of obstacles such as jumps, weaves, A-frames and tunnels. They follow their owners' instructions to find the correct route on a course. This meant a whole new dictionary of commands to learn, both for us and our puppies, as well as learning how to train a dog to do the variety of obstacles.

Our dog agility career began in an outside arena about the size of two netball pitches and completely enclosed by six- to eight-foot-high chain-link fencing. At least there was no chance of our dogs running off to the neighbouring woods. The flooring was bare earth, which became quite muddy close to the contact equipment, especially after rain. In the arena were all the obstacles that were used for dog agility. A selection of jumps included a long jump, a tunnel, a tyre, weaving poles and then the 'contact' equipment – the A-frame, dog walk and seesaw. The bottom two- to three-foot section of these obstacles is painted a different colour from the main part, and the dogs must touch this area with at least one paw when going up and coming down the equipment. Enthusiastic dogs could easily injure themselves if they leapt off the equipment from too far up.

Rudge and Rolo, in true Labrador style, enjoyed themselves and fairly quickly learnt to do all the obstacles. As owners we were encouraged to see our dogs use their intelligence and really enjoy themselves on the course. Nula, the golden retriever, had a very different mindset. She soon decided that it wasn't really her idea of fun and simply refused to enter into the spirit of the game however hard she was encouraged. She had had a similar attitude to being a guide dog, hence her need for a career change. Her owner gave up after a few weeks of trying.

Although Rolo enjoyed doing agility, he only stayed for one term. As a pup he had had major surgery on his hind legs and it was felt that agility could easily cause him more problems in that area, so Rudge was the only one of the three beginners to continue with a career as an agility dog.

There was no training at this arena during the winter. Because I was enjoying this new challenge and so was Rudge, I looked for a new venue. I joined Cranbourne Agility Club, which met on Thursday evenings all year round at the indoor riding arena at the Berkshire College of Agriculture in Maidenhead – quite a contrast to our original venue. It had a sandy floor, overhead lighting and shelter from all weathers, although on a cold night it was worth wearing at least two or three warm jumpers. We soon slotted into this new club and both made new two- and four-legged friends.

Rudge proved to be very steady in the winter league competitions that we entered; although not fast, he achieved many clear rounds and points for the club. I was quite glad that he wasn't a fast dog. Looking at the pace of some of the other dogs, especially the border collies, I wasn't sure I would have been able to keep up with him had he been running any faster. He even earned himself the title of 'Reliable Rudge' and one year won the trophy for the steadiest dog. I was a very proud owner that year.

Rudge particularly enjoyed our holidays, either staying in a cottage and walking in the surrounding area or, better still, a canal boat holiday. He definitely seemed to think he was one of the crew. His agility skills came in useful when he had to get on and off the boat. He could easily jump from the stern of the boat onto the bank. It was bit more difficult to get on and off the boat at the bow, but we all found that a problem. We usually had to step over the side of the boat and onto the side benches and then down onto the foredeck. Sometimes, the only way to get on and off the boat was via a gangplank, with one end on the boat and the other on the towpath. Walking the gangplank was where Rudge's agility training really came into its own, although even he was a bit hesitant, like the rest of the crew, when the plank wobbled.

Rudge instinctively knew that the rules were different on a boat. When I sat on one of the side benches at the front, he would get up and sit next to me, and yet at home he would never attempt to join me on the settee. David liked to sit straddling the bow of the boat with his legs hanging down either side. Rudge was only too happy to sit in front of Dave on the small area of deck that was left. Not many boats have a chocolate Labrador for a figurehead. I'm sure many dogs travel on the bow of the boat or the bench seat, but Rudge's attitude never seemed to be 'doggy'. He would never choose to sit in either of these places unless he was accompanied by an adult. He always seemed to be copying the person he was with and with an attitude that made me think that he thought he was a human being.

In June, six months after Rudge returned to the fold, Rebel was a year old and went to kennels to be trained as a guide dog. He qualified after nine months and was a guide for a lady who lived in

Rudge, the canal boat figurehead

Kent. Now we were down to three dogs, a better number to cope with than four, but not for much longer. Gazza was ageing, already deaf and nearly blind, plus he was beginning to lose control of his bladder as well as his bowels. He still had a good appetite and enjoyed life, but I had to be very alert to make sure he could get to the toileting area quickly. I find it hard to make the decision to say that enough is enough, especially when a dog is still happy, but I always try and convince myself and my friends, when they are in the same situation, that we will know when that time comes. Sure enough, one morning in September when I came downstairs,

Gazza didn't greet me. He was in a bit of a mess and didn't want food. It was time to call it a day.

The following day, I phoned Gazza's owner to let her know that I had had him put to sleep the day before, 6th September. Although she hadn't seen Gazza for over a year I thought she would appreciate knowing that he had died. During the conversation it emerged that, coincidently, that was the very date that she had qualified with Gazza thirteen years earlier. It was probably a good job that I hadn't known that fact the day before.

Rehomed Dogs United

David was inspired to write the following article on behalf of Rudge.

On 25th August 1995 I was brought into this world. My mother had visions of me becoming a champion gun dog but, after six weeks, I decided I'd leave home and train as a guide dog. After a happy year with the Eastons, I went to further my education. Sadly, the high level of concentration needed was beyond me. I briefly looked at a career as a sniffer dog and Dogs for the Disabled, but I was just too sensitive for the pressure of this work. Therefore, I took the redundancy package from Guide Dogs and returned to the Easton household as an assistant puppy-walker. The task seemed to be ideal: a walk in the morning before work and then a busy day of playing, eating and sleeping. In my spare time I enjoy playing 'hide-and-seek' with my toys. But my main passion is 'agility'. I practise once a week, but only at an elementary level, and find the exercise very good for my figure.

By Reliable Rudge
(with a little help from David Easton –
son of the puppy-walker)

Like a duck
takes to water

We were always open to trying new animal ventures and our friends were only too willing to encourage us. One morning I received a phone call from my friend who lived nearby. She and her husband were also into country living and had a very productive garden. They had kept quails and bees, and had friends with a smallholding that they helped to look after. Knowing how much David enjoyed animals, she made us an offer I couldn't refuse. "Would David like some fertile Cayuga duck eggs to hatch?" We had no idea what a Cayuga duck was like, but if we hatched the eggs we'd soon find out. Perhaps I should have done a little homework before I said yes. Up to this time, David had only used his incubator to hatch quail eggs, so duck eggs were a whole new ball game. We all wanted to be involved, so David brought the incubator into the kitchen where we could follow the events.

David had a proven track record for successfully hatching quails' eggs and so was in charge of running the incubator, making sure it was kept at the right temperature and humidity and that the eggs were turning. We had several books about caring for poultry, but the one we now needed was the one that referred to hatching and rearing birds – in particular, ducks. We discovered that they take twenty-eight days to hatch and need a slightly higher humidity than quail eggs. David set everything up and we settled down to wait.

For three and a half weeks there was nothing to see; everything was happening inside the egg, hopefully. At twenty-five days the turner was switched off and the plastic strips which stopped the eggs from rolling around were removed. This is when things became exciting. Eggs with live birds inside occasionally rock gently when the chick moves. It was very much a case of 'blink and you'll miss it'. On day twenty-eight, four of the five eggs began to hatch. It started with the ducklings pecking a small hole in the shell. This is called

Cayuga ducklings enjoy a swim

'pipping'. Eventually, after about three hours, the shells cracked all the way round like a lid, and wet black ducklings emerged. After twenty-four hours they had dried out and were now black and fluffy and about the same size as a gerbil, much bigger than anything else we had hatched, which was a bit worrying. We moved them to the brooder, which again was the large fish tank with a red lightbulb suspended from the lid, to keep them warm. It wasn't necessary to keep moving it up as we usually did, as the ducklings were too big to have it any lower. Every morning we took them out and played with them on the kitchen floor. A large towel, a bowl of water and four ducklings made compulsive viewing. They had fun running around the floor and swimming in their bowl of water. The saying 'like a duck takes to water' is so true. They grew very quickly but kept their downy feathers for some time, as opposed to chicks, which don't seem to grow very quickly but start to grow proper feathers after a few days.

These ducks were named after characters from the children's television programme, *Trumpton*. We had Hugh, Pugh, Barney McGrew and Dibble. We couldn't use the name Cuthbert because we already had a quail by that name. Always happy to show our pets to friends, we soon had a visit from the neighbours who had sold us our Silver Appleyard ducks. They were much more knowledgeable about ducks than us and pointed out that adult Cayuga ducks are black and weigh about eight pounds. They would grow to be a similar size to a Canada goose and we all knew how big they were. At the time, our Silver Appleyard ducks weighed about one and a half pounds each, so we could have an overcrowding problem on our hands in a few months' time. Still, we could cross that bridge when we got to it; the interest they provided as we watched them grow definitely made up for an overcrowding problem to sort out later.

As they grew, we found we had three drakes and one female duck – Dibble was the female. When they were old enough, David entered two of them,

Hugh and Dibble, a breeding pair, in the Henley Agricultural Show. He won a second prize with Hugh and a 'best in show' with them as a pair of ducks – very good for a first attempt.

Chris and David had taken the ducks to Henley in the morning, but David couldn't come back to get them later in the day because he was still working at the Animal Rescue Centre on Saturdays. Chris and I were tasked with returning to the show to collect the birds, and decided to spend his winnings, on his behalf, on some chicken feed; they needed to start earning their keep. David had agreed that we could sell Hugh and Dibble as we really hadn't got space for all the Cayuga ducks at home and, as the prize-winning 'best in show' birds, it wasn't long before someone showed an interest and bought them from us. I felt quite sad parting with them and I just hoped they would be cared for as well as they had been with us.

Now we had more money to spend and were loose in a bird-lovers' paradise. We had no room for more ducks, but bantams were a different proposition. There are some interesting breeds around and we were attracted to some French Faverolles. They are a mixture of browns, fawns and beiges with feathery legs, and the cock has iridescent green tail feathers. So we bought a trio: one cock and two hens. We felt sure Dave would love them, which he did, but he would have been just as happy with the cash as his pocket money didn't go very far. Ultimately we were the financial losers. Our resident hens, and in particular our cockerel, were not at all impressed with sharing their house and run with the Faverolles. We had to buy another chicken house and section off part of the main run for the new bantams. That was our comeuppance for spending David's earnings without his permission.

Bracken, all action dog

At home I consider my working day to be from 7am when I get up until 7pm after our evening meal. From then until bedtime it is 'me' time, to do what I want to do to relax. This could be sewing, knitting, doing a jigsaw puzzle or even just watching TV. I have to bend my rules when a new six-week-old puppy arrives. They have four feeds a day: 8am, 12 noon, 4pm and 8pm. By the time the pup has eaten its 8pm meal, been to the toilet and had a little play, it is nearly 9pm – not much 'me' time left. I don't like to wish the puppy's life away, but I am so pleased when it reaches twelve weeks old. Then it goes on to three meals a day, the last one being at 6pm, so by 7pm puppy is ready for a quiet evening asleep and I can do my own thing.

Not so with Bracken, my sixteenth puppy, a golden retriever crossed with a Labrador. He was a good-looking dog and had a lot of energy, which needed to be channelled in the right direction. He was always willing to work, but unfortunately this enthusiasm carried on into the evening until way after the initial six weeks. It took a bit of time for me to convince him that I was off duty after 7pm and it was my time to relax. He found it impossible to lie quietly next to me on a lead. He insisted on chewing the lead or nibbling my feet or shoes, even though he had a selection of toys and a chew to keep him occupied. He would have been a lot happier going for yet another training walk down the road to the post box and back, but I wasn't. He was what I called 'my twenty-four-hour-a-day dog', as that was how long he was prepared to keep going.

He also had a stubborn streak, which would appear occasionally, and definitely if we were going out to drive somewhere in my little red Volkswagen Polo. I always chose my cars for their dog friendliness. They have to be a hatchback and, if possible, have a totally flat back floor when the seats are lowered. I have had car salesmen who were very keen to tell me all about the engine capacity and driving capability of the vehicle, when I am far more interested in the layout of the back. It seemed Bracken was even pickier about cars than I was.

He would never jump into the back of the car; he would carefully put his front feet on the sill and then patiently wait for me to lift him up instead. No amount of cajoling or encouragement could get him to change his mind; I think he had delusions of grandeur.

One day, I had taken Bracken and Rudge for a free run through the parkland on the edge of the village. We had had a fair amount of wintery rain that week and, although spring was well on its way, the rain had left its usual collection of surface water for us all to enjoy. At about halfway round our usual circuit, Rudge's favourite rubber ball bounced into an area of deep muddy water, so he went to get it, something he would have managed quite easily on his own. Unfortunately, Bracken decided to help, and joined in the search, but without any focus or direction, just leaping about aimlessly in the muddy water, stirring up the dirt and ruining any chance of Rudge ever finding his ball. Eventually I realised that Bracken was not going to stop helping and, with the water now so disturbed, Rudge had no chance of performing his usual magic. Reluctantly I called both dogs to me and abandoned all hope of getting the ball back, and we continued on our final section of the walk.

When we got back to the car, Rudge jumped in as usual, but Bracken took his favoured stance, front feet on the lip of the boot, head in the air looking around him, just waiting for me to perform 'my duty' and lift him into the car. Now, one thing I really hate doing is getting myself dirty, and at this point I refused to even consider getting covered in Bracken's surplus mud in order for him to get into the back of the car. As I was also rather cross that he had been the reason for losing Rudge's ball he had absolutely no chance of a lift. The turning point had been reached and in this scenario I was definitely going to be more stubborn than my dog, even if we were there for the rest of the morning. After considering the situation, I decided to put Bracken on his lead, walk about fifteen yards away from the open hatch of the car and then run back at a fast pace, hoping that this would give him enough momentum to launch himself up and into the back. With a bit of help from me and the lead, it worked. Bracken learnt a big lesson that day, as from then on he was quite happy to jump into the back of my car, and he didn't even need a long run to do it.

Bracken's time with us passed uneventfully. He was a quick learner and a natural guide dog, easily acquiring all the skills required of him to do the job well, as well as developing a few distinctive habits that set him apart from our other puppies, one of which was collecting rather large sticks. When he was on a free run, Bracken would find a piece of wood – anything from six feet long by one and a half inches in diameter to two feet long but at least three inches in diameter – that he was prepared to carry for the whole length of a walk, which could be anything up to an hour. These were heavy hunks of timber, so he must have had a really strong jaw. We ended up with quite a collection that he brought home from free runs, which were all piled up to the left of the back door.

A few weeks before Bracken left us I took him with me into Reading to buy a wedding present. I parked in a two-hour parking space about three-quarters of a mile from the shop, giving Bracken a route to walk that gradually got busier. When I reached the shop I wanted, I discovered that the wedding present department was on the first floor. The lifts and stairs were at the back of the shop and to get there we had to zig zag quite a bit to get around the various stands and counters. Once on the first floor, we crossed the shop again and arrived at the wedding service counter, having followed quite a circuitous route.

I had perused the list earlier and decided to buy sheets, as they would fit snugly into my dog friendly rucksack, leaving me two free hands to hold the lead and control the dog on the return journey. Unfortunately, someone else had already bought them, so I had to choose a different present. On an impulse I decided to buy some pillows; they were the right price and would go with the sheets that someone else had now bought. I paid for them, but as the staff put the pillows into a large carrier bag I realised that I had made a mistake. The two pillows would never fit into my small rucksack, which meant I would have to carry the large bulk of pillows in my right hand whilst holding Bracken's lead in my left hand. Not textbook puppy-walking technique but, in theory, it works; as long as the dog isn't distracted, two hands aren't needed on the lead.

Thinking on my feet, I decided to get back down to the ground floor with both the newly acquired pillows and an enthusiastic dog, leave the pillows with a member of staff on a counter near the main exit (I couldn't leave the dog) and walk back to the car with Bracken. I could then leave him safely in the back of the car and retrace my steps to collect the pillows. As the car was at least a fifteen-minute walk away from the shop, I consoled myself with the fact that it would all be good exercise for me, and so set off across the shop floor.

As I walked back through the shop I quickly realised that Bracken was taking control of the situation and leading me through the shop along exactly the same zig zag path that we had come in. In fact, he was remembering the route far better than me. By the time we reached the main entrance, I was so enjoying watching him work and so intrigued by how he would cope with the rest of the walk that I changed my plan and decided to go back to the car with both dog and pillows. If an emergency struck and all else failed, I could just drop the pillows, leaving both hands free to control Bracken.

This turned out to be one of the best decisions I have made. Bracken was in guide dog mode. I asked him to 'Find the car' and off he went, again following in reverse the exact route we had walked about an hour earlier. He was so honed in on the job that he wasn't distracted by anything. I don't think he would even have noticed a pack of dogs if they had appeared. During our walk back, the sky gradually got darker and darker, then, just as we got in the car about fifteen minutes later, the heavens opened and it began to pour with rain. I rapidly bundled Bracken into the back, threw the pillows onto the back seat, flung open the driver's door and leapt in as fast as I could. I was now doubly pleased with my decision; not only had I had the pleasure of seeing my confident dog work well, but I would have been drenched if I had had to go back to the shop to collect the pillows.

A few weeks later Bracken left us to be trained as a guide dog. I think he was a natural, really. He qualified and went to work in Surrey with a man who subsequently kept us informed of Bracken's life with him. We were lucky enough to be able to board him a couple of times when his owner went on holiday. It's always lovely to have your pup back for a week or two to see what a responsible dog they have become, but also to see how many of their puppy traits they have retained. From our first walk out with Bracken when we boarded him, it was clear that stick carrying was a habit he had continued into his working life. Within moments of being off the lead he had found his chosen branch and remained attached to it for the remainder of the walk. I was very glad to welcome the back door stick collection again, if only for a fortnight.

Bracken's owner also loved his stick carrying habit and one year produced a calendar with pictures of Bracken carrying sticks he had collected, a different one for every month of the year. There were thin ones, thick ones, straight ones, bendy ones, ones that could almost be classed as logs, and the most impressive, a seven-foot branch, which he had carefully balanced in his mouth. How they got that one home safely I shall never know.

Between Pups

There were puppy-free times when we were able to get the house back in order. The next poem reflects that.

I've polished the silver and cleaned the brass,
We've cut the hedge and mown the grass.
I've visited aunts I don't often see
And invited friends round for cups of tea.
I've filled in a tax form and written letters,
We've cleaned the windows and emptied gutters.
We've painted the landing, stairs and hall;
We've sanded and cleaned and treated the floor.
Our carpets aren't shredded, nor are our shoes,
There aren't any 'puddles' or any 'poos'.
I've been out shopping for ever so long;
I've had time to look and try things on.
I can go when it's hot and park in the sun
It doesn't matter 'cos the pup hasn't come.
There aren't any shops that I can't go in;
Shopping is much easier without HIM.
I've time on my hands, so I'm going to classes,
Learning to arrange flowers in vases.
The badminton racket is out again
And now I'm complaining of aches and pains.
The patchwork group is much more relaxing;
There's not much sewing, it's mainly chatting.

I've sat in the evening and watched TV
Without getting up to let puppy 'pee'.
I've watched a video from beginning to end
Without having to 'pause' to let puppy 'spend'.
The big dogs can last an evening's viewing
Without getting up for 'piddling' and 'pooing'.
Puppy-walkers are voluntary, always on call.
I hope someone appreciates it all.
A lady rang the other day:
"I'm Lorraine, with Rebel," I heard her say.
"He's a lovely dog and his work is good
And I'd like to thank you for all you did."

So perhaps the hassle was all worthwhile;
I phoned my supervisor and said with a smile…

"ANOTHER PUP, PLEASE!!"

By Monica Easton

Gibson, the
relaxed recruit

Bracken left us, but the next pup soon followed, and one from the same bloodline. Gibson was another golden retriever crossed with a Labrador, and half-brother to Bracken; they both had the same dad, a golden retriever called Floyd; but that was where the similarities ended. Bracken was golden and stubborn, but Gibson was black and a really laid-back puppy. He took life in a very casual manner. He did everything in his own time and he wasn't going to be rushed into anything. He walked at a steady pace, but to heel and not leading out. Although I must admit that it was good not to have my left arm nearly pulled out of its socket, if he was going to make it as a guide dog he would have to walk ahead with his hind legs level with my legs. I had spent so long trying to stop puppies from pulling that a whole new set of skills had to be applied in order to encourage Gibson to walk ahead of me. A fluffy toy dangled in front of him and an excited voice from me helped a bit, but he was never going to pull.

All was going well in a 'laid-back Gibson' kind of a way until at four months old Gibson, now nicknamed Gibby, became ill with doggy sickness and diarrhoea. It started in the usual way, but then seemed more serious than a bout caused by eating something unsavoury. I was really worried about him. He didn't want any food and wouldn't get out of bed; even for my laid-back puppy this was not normal. I decided that a visit to the vet was needed. Even though it was a Bank Holiday I felt it couldn't wait. Why do they always seem to be ill on a Bank Holiday? The vet was also worried. He prescribed a course of antibiotics and then talked about other things that it could be and suggested several tests. Thankfully my common sense took over. "Let's try the antibiotics and see how he responds." This turned out to be a wise decision. After a couple of days he was back to his usual laid-back self. I think the severity of his symptoms were indicative of doggy 'man' flu rather than some terrible disease and he just felt sorry for himself.

Gibson had a long-lasting impact on the Easton household and to this day his name is remembered whenever I feed the dogs in our now very smartly revamped utility room. When we had Miffy and puppies at the same time, she was allowed to have her food in a small metal bowl that was kept on the work surface in the utility room. That way she could eat her food when she wanted it, leave it when she didn't and the dogs couldn't help themselves to it. This system worked well for all our puppies, including Gibby, until he reached nine to ten months old. By this time, being a large, long-legged dog, he found he could, with no effort at all, jump up, put his two front feet on the work surface and reach Miffy's food at the back. Being a polite dog, he wouldn't take it while she was eating but, if left there during the day, he helped himself to whatever was left when no one was looking. I watched him once over the stable door gently put his paws on the work surface, turn his head and deftly clear the bowl in a matter of seconds. I pulled him up on this bad behaviour, but he was unrepentant. Something needed to be done. To solve the problem, Chris made a shelf and put it on the wall over the sink, just above my head height. Then, if Miffy didn't eat all her food, I could put her bowl on the shelf and get it down for her when she came back later. This seemed to work well for all parties and has now become a bit of an institution. The shelf was named

'Gibby's shelf' and to this day is a useful place for keeping a few special dog treats on. As I write I can see an animal hide bone and several dog chews all ready for the next dog who earns them.

Gibby qualified very quickly; he holds the record for being the fastest qualifier I have walked, and he went to work with a blind man in Sussex. His owner telephoned me not long after qualifying with Gibby, and during our conversation I mentioned the shelf. By this time, I had learnt that a dog really doesn't change its habits. Later on, I heard that Gibby had transferred his skills to a new location and was helping himself to food from the back of the work surface in his new home. There was now another Gibby shelf, this time in West Sussex.

Once again we were lucky that Gibby's owner kept in contact with us, and we had the pleasure of boarding Gibby, and Jenna, Gibby's owner's wife's guide dog, on two or three occasions when they went on holiday. I enjoy ex-pupils coming to stay and I think my own dogs do too. Apart from them having some different playmates, we also make an effort to take them on different, interesting, free run walks every day, which we all benefit from. When Gibby came to stay, our treat walk was along the towpath next to the River Thames near Shiplake lock. At that time there was a tea garden at the lock. Walking the dogs along the river, followed by cup of tea and piece of cake out in the open air, watching the boats travel through the lock, was time very well spent.

When Gibson retired at about nine and a half years old I was asked if I would be able to have him back. Sadly, I had to refuse as we already had retired Jake, rehomed Rudge and the inevitable puppy. I was relieved when I heard that Gibby was going to be rehomed with a friend of his owner who lived in the same town. At least it would be a bit easier for the two of them to meet up occasionally.

Jake, the 'best man'

Alastair, Jake's owner, came to visit us on several occasions, bringing Jake with him. In true guide dog fashion, Jake ignored us when he was working in harness, but when he was off the lead he relaxed and was the same fun-loving Jake that we knew. We also boarded Jake a few times when his owner went on holiday. One of the most memorable of these occasions was when Alastair and his wife went on honeymoon.

Chris and I were invited to the wedding, which was in Paisley Abbey near Glasgow. It was definitely not a day trip, so we drove north on the Friday and stayed in the hotel where the reception was to be held. This gave us an opportunity to meet some of the other wedding guests who were also staying at the hotel.

It was an April wedding, and Saturday morning began with true April showers, Scottish style, but that didn't dampen anybody's spirits. We waited in the foyer with all the other guests, to catch the bus that had been arranged to transport everyone from the hotel to the abbey. That way there was no worry about following directions or parking our car, and we were all dry on arrival, in spite of the weather.

Paisley Abbey is a large twelfth-century classic church building about twelve miles from the centre of Glasgow. So that the guests could see the ceremony, we were ushered into the choir stalls in the chancel. Even that area was larger than our local church. There were two rows of choir stalls on either side. We sat on the right-hand side in the back row. The groom and best man arrived at the abbey, both wearing kilts. I shouldn't have been surprised considering the Scottish connections of the bride and groom. Jake arrived with them, looking to all intents and purposes as though he thought he was the 'best man'.

The bride, Anne, arrived a few minutes later looking very elegant in a long white satin dress and carrying a bouquet of white lilies and roses. To complete the picture were two adult bridesmaids wearing mid-blue satin dresses.

After the ceremony the bride and groom walked back down the wide central aisle past the choir stalls.

This is where Jake was most certainly the 'best' dog, if not the 'best man', as he confidently guided his master and bride down the centre of the chancel. What impressed me was the fact that Jake went in such a straight line. Generally, the bride and groom walk down the narrow aisle of the church with the ends of pews either side to dictate the route, but this was like walking down the centre of a road, so there were no close reference points for him to use.

Jake was on his master's left-hand side, which meant he was on the same side as the choir stalls where we were sitting. I'm sure he knew we were there, as he glanced to the left and did a little wag of his tail as he passed, but didn't let himself be distracted any more than that as he was aware of the important job he was doing.

Things were more relaxed in the shelter of the stone cloisters on the outside of the abbey building. With Jake off duty I went over to say hello. I was greeted by a very excited thirty-kilogram Labrador who, for a couple of minutes, was almost uncontrollable. He was so pleased to see me, and even recognised me in my posh clothes, not my usual jeans that seem to be my puppy-walking uniform. I could tell that he was going to enjoy the day just as much as everyone else.

At the reception, the room was laid out with a head table for the wedding party and several smaller tables for the guests, each seating about eight people.

The head table was covered with a cloth, which was gathered at the top edge and went down to floor level. This is where the bride's guide dog Kai put in an appearance. Lying under the table she managed to ease herself forward, and finished up with her head and shoulders into the main part of the room, with the lower edge of the tablecloth draping neatly across her back. Now it was her turn to be part of the party.

The following day the newlyweds were flying across the Atlantic for a two-week honeymoon in the United States. Needless to say, Jake wasn't going with them. I don't think all the hustle and bustle would have been his idea of a holiday anyway. He spent two weeks in Berkshire with us and his friend Rudge, with plenty of free runs in woods, fields and along the Thames towpath – an ideal holiday for a guide dog.

Polecats as pets

I n the background, our household pets were keeping us just as busy as the puppies. In particular, the polecats, Columbus and Midge, provided loads of entertainment. They are busy and inquisitive animals that need lots of action to keep them occupied. Pleased with his new pets, David had made them a large run which was attached to the back of an old rabbit hutch. He had made a pop-hole at the back of the hutch to allow the two animals easy access to the run, but which could also be closed off, leaving them outside and giving us unfettered access to their living quarters. It was useful to be able to shut the polecats out to have fun in the open area, and then be able to access the hutch to clean it out without two inquisitive, lively animals to 'help' with the job or, worse still, escape. David had made the run, which was about three feet wide, six feet long and eighteen inches high, into an adventure playground. It contained flexible drainage pipes, an old watering can, several platforms to climb on, a small ladder and a ball for them to push around. They loved it.

Although siblings, the two polecats were very different characters. Columbus was a fairly laid-back animal; Midge, on the other hand, was lively and a busybody. They had fun chasing each other all over their adventure playground. Midge usually managed to run faster and get into smaller spaces, as she was much quicker and almost half the size of Columbus. He would follow her around, but gave up the chase when things got too difficult for him.

Feeding time was also fun as both animals had a different approach to food. Columbus simply went to the bowl and ate. Midge was much more concerned about keeping something for later. She would get some food, take it away and hide it in a secret place. I think her idea was that she could get it and eat it later at her leisure, or perhaps it was a motherly instinct and she was storing food for the family, which she hadn't got. Columbus always seemed to find these secret hiding places, and when his bowl of food was empty he casually sauntered off to the stored food and either ate it or brought it back to the bowl, much to Midge's frustration as she had to start all over again.

I enjoyed watching these two animals' fun and active approach to life, but most definitely from outside the safe confines of the cage. Dave, on the other hand, was keen to take them out. Each week he would open up the garage and sideway, shut the doors to the garden and kitchen, then bring them in for a free run in a larger space. The two would hare up and down the floor, and as quick as lightning they would be into wellington boots, clambering onto the top of surfaces or climbing David's trouser legs.

Columbus, checking out a wellington boot

Polecats can also be trained to walk on a lead, which David was keen to try. He invested in a small harness for each animal that went in an x-shape around each of their front legs, meeting again at the top where the thin leather lead could be attached. They were always excited when he got the leads out, and how he managed to attach them with these wiry creatures jumping up and continually wriggling I don't know, but he did, and quite quickly too. David would then set out up the drive and along the pavement towards the little shop, allowing them to have a good sniff and investigate all the interesting smells along the way. I'm not sure they got very far, as polecats find everything interesting, and they certainly wouldn't have passed the guide dog requirement of walking in a straight line down the road, but they had a lot of fun together.

One winter evening when I came back from dog agility with Rudge, I had a phone call from the next-door neighbour to say that Midge was in their garden. By this time Columbus had died and we only had Midge to look after. It was inevitable that she would escape sometime, but David wasn't around that evening; the Polecat rescue expedition fell to me and I really wasn't sure how I was going to manage it. The first rule of lifesaving is to keep the life saver safe so, strange as it may seem, my first priority was to shut the pop-hole to the chicken house in case I had a visit from a fox and then no longer had any hens as well as an escaped polecat. It also gave me a bit of thinking time to decide how to catch a free running polecat. Inspiration came as I remembered that Lucy, Midge's mother, had responded instantly to her babies squealing. I grabbed one of the dog's squeaky toys and went next door to see if Midge would come to me when I squeaked it. It worked. Midge came to me straight away. I put her into a carry cage for safety and then inspected the hutch and the run to find and repair the hole through which she had escaped.

Going away on holiday became quite interesting once we had the polecats. At this time Julie was still living at home but no longer coming away with us. While we were away she was happy to look after our, by now quite large, menagerie and the vegetable garden. The first time we were all away when the polecats were there she valiantly agreed to look after them, but I knew that she was even more concerned about their speed and sharp teeth than I was and would find it daunting. And what would happen if they escaped whilst she was in charge? She was not a natural with polecats, and so in the end we decided we needed to find someone else to look after them.

Asking someone to look after a pet cat or a guinea pig is easy. Often parents are glad for their children to have the chance to look after animals without owning one. It's also quite a simple matter to find someone to look after a coop full of chickens, as long as you don't have a broody hen to deal with; but a polecat is another matter.

After a lot of asking around, Julie only had to look after them for two days and could fill up their food and water bowl through the cage door. One of David's colleagues from the Animal Rescue Centre came and collected them. He already had a polecat of his own, so was quite happy to look after ours for the rest of the week. I think Julie was very relieved as they were driven away that her responsibility towards them had ended.

Fenton, the agoraphobic pup

Pure-bred Labradors are one of the breeds of dog frequently used by Guide Dogs, so it really was unusual when, for me, a yellow Labrador had become 'something different'. Fenton was a yellow Labrador, my first for ten years. Varley had shown such strange behaviour traits that I had tarred all yellow Labradors with the same brush and had thus far managed to avoid having another one. The time had come to put all those fears to the back of my mind, and so the small, pale, wiry Fenton came to stay with us. His dad was Guide Dogs stock, but his mum was outside-bred. There was nothing wrong with that; Jake could claim the same type of breeding and he was a brilliant dog. It wasn't long before my fears about a yellow Labrador began to resurface.

For the first few days with us he behaved like any other pup, eating, sleeping and playing in a good routine throughout the day. He was happy to go into the garden to spend, and fitted in well with our other pets. The change came when I took Fenton out to the front of the house for a short walk, or at least attempted to. He had been so good since he had arrived that I was completely taken by surprise when his ears went back, his eyes grew wide and he pulled back into the house, stretching to the end of the lead. "Come on then, Fenton, good boy," I said in my most encouraging tone of voice. He was reluctant to walk, but this was not unusual, after all, he was only eight weeks old, so I picked him up to carry him and continued out of the house. This usually solved the problem, as most pups are quite happy to be cuddled and would then relax in this situation, but not Fenton. For the whole of our short walk he remained tense and even tried to scrabble up and climb over my shoulder. It was quite hard keeping hold of him, he was wriggling so much. I was afraid I was going to drop him. The moment we were back home and indoors, Fenton relaxed. This was something unusual in my experience that would require a lot of patience to overcome.

We started small. For the next few days I just carried Fenton a few yards down our road. I couldn't go far as he was struggling so hard in my arms and trying to climb over my shoulder again. I began to wonder if perhaps he did want to walk after all, so I put him on the pavement to walk to my next-door neighbour, who always liked to see my puppies and was happy to be part of any training plan, but that didn't work either. Fenton just ran to the end of the lead and tried to hide in the bottom of her large laurel hedge, looking terrified. In the end, I just held him and stood in our driveway to get him used to the outside world, but still he wasn't relaxed.

It was obvious that Fenton was a puppy with a problem, and identifying it was going to be my challenge. I already knew that he definitely didn't like tarmac roads and pavements, with or without vehicles on them. Also he didn't want to venture out onto our gravel driveway, although he was quite happy to go into the back garden, on to the patio and lawn.

He didn't like cars going along the road, but fortunately was happy to travel in one. My car was usually parked by the side of the house on the gravel driveway, and Fenton would run from the back door and jump quickly into the back, a complete contrast from my earlier dog Bracken. If I hadn't got the hatch open in time he would dive underneath the car and hide, terrified, until the door was open, and then jump in, desperate for the safety of the car. This meant he usually had oily streaks somewhere on his body.

One of our favourite walks is along the Thames towpath from Shiplake towards Reading. We decided to take Fenton for a walk there so that he could enjoy a walk by the river through grassy fields and along the towpath by the grassy banks without having to go along much tarmac or outdoor space to get there. I did have to carry him a short distance, about one hundred yards, from the car along a narrow country lane. Once at the towpath there was only a large field to walk through next to the river. That was fine, or it would have been if there hadn't been any boats on the river. We hadn't been there for long when a small boat motored past us towards the lock. Fenton panicked and we had to wait until it had gone past. He continued to panic whenever a boat went by and, after about 200 yards, we abandoned the walk and went back to the car with a very frightened pup. At this point, his eyes were bulging and his ears were right back. Between us we carried him most of the way to the car, which was no mean feat as he was about four months old by this time and getting quite heavy. So we had discovered that rivers and boats caused the same problem as cars and tarmac. It was very sad.

Soon after this incident we went on holiday and Fenton was boarded by my supervisor so that she could see his problems for herself. She noticed all the things that I had mentioned to her, including occasionally being sick and being reluctant to eat. When I got back from holiday I had a phone call from her to say that Fenton would need a career change. She asked if I would be willing to have him back for a few months until he was old enough to be rehomed. He would be treated as a pet at this stage and I need only take him to areas where he was happy and certainly with no more road walking. Our focus changed and it was a relief not to have to try and conquer Fenton's problems, but instead try and work out how to enable him to live a happy life. From now on we could avoid all situations that would worry him.

I still encountered a few incidents, though. One that stands out in my mind is when Julie asked me to take him to the school where she taught, and give a talk to the children about training guide dog puppies. The school backed onto the local recreation ground, which meant that I could park my car in the car park and walk Fenton across the grassy area, arriving at the back of the school and directly into Julie's classroom. There was no way he would have been able to walk along the pavement from the school car park to the main entrance. I pulled my car up, with the bonnet next to the edge of the field, and opened the back of the car so that Fenton could get out. Immediately his ears went down, his eyes bulged and he got as far away from me as possible. Thinking quickly, I closed the door, turned the car round and parked it with the back facing the playing fields. This time when I lifted the hatchback door he happily got out of the car and came to me. This event really highlighted to me the severity of his fear of tarmac. With the boot facing the tarmac car park he was completely traumatised; the moment his view was of the field, he came out of the car a happy dog with his tail high and nose sniffing the breeze.

Fenton happily walked the 200 yards across the playing field to the school gate, but then he froze. He would have to walk across about ten yards of tarmac path to get to the classroom, which completely panicked him. I didn't want to go home at this stage; Julie had seen us and opened the door in preparation. With the classroom door now open, he could see a bolthole. With some dragging from me at first, he then ran for the safety of the room. Once inside, Fenton was a model dog. He lay down quietly by my feet while I gave my talk, and was quite happy to be stroked by any of the children. On our return, he had to make another mad dash to the gate of the playing field, but after that he was happy to walk back across the field to the car. It seemed to me that he was displaying all the same problems as a person with agoraphobia.

I kept Fenton until he was ten months old. During this time with me as a career-change dog, I only ever took him for free runs, but even some of those could be a challenge. I could never walk him from home, I always had to take him in the car to a free run area. One of my regular local walks meant parking my car at the edge of the road and doing a circular walk; well, a square walk, really. The first side of the route was always along a concrete track that ran parallel to the main railway route to London. That section was fine; why he was happy to walk along a concrete path but not a gravel or tarmac one I shall never know, and the trains never bothered him. The second side went through rough ground and long grass, which was also OK. The third side was along the edge of a recreation ground, but heading towards the road. As he got nearer to the road he began to panic and started to run, so it was at this stage that I had to put him on the lead. The first time this happened I didn't realise what he was going to do. I called him back to me, but he was in such a state that he wouldn't come and just ran headlong towards the road. I was afraid that he would get run over by a car and raced after him as quickly as I could. I shouldn't have worried. Once I got up to the road, there he was, hiding under my car, trembling. My first feeling was one of relief that he was in one piece as I went about opening the hatch and coaxing him out from under the car and into his safe space, but it also highlighted how even a free run was difficult for him and I was very sad that he couldn't enjoy it. Even on a lead, he never enjoyed that fourth side of the walk, although it was through long grass separated from the road by a thick hedge. He always pulled all the way back to the car and only relaxed when he was safely inside it. Fenton was rehomed when he was ten months old to a couple who lived in the New Forest and already had another career-change guide dog to keep him company. Their house backed onto an expanse of open ground, so he could enjoy a free run without ever having to go near a car or tarmac. The perfect place for him.

Ingle, Miss Impetuous

"Would you be able to look after a seven-week-old puppy until a permanent puppy-walker has been found for her?" came the early morning call from my supervisor. The puppy was a yellow Labrador bitch called Ingle. She had been placed with a first-time puppy-walker the previous week, but unfortunately she was no longer able to look after her because circumstances had changed. Despite my initial preference for a bitch when I had started to puppy-walk, by this time I had reached the point where I preferred to walk dogs, but I was quite prepared to look after a bitch for a few days.

Happy to help out, I took delivery of Ingle the

following day. Her personality was quite a contrast to Fenton's; 'much more exuberant' was putting it mildly. When she arrived, Rudge was having a quiet nap in his bed and was not at all enthusiastic about another pup disturbing his peace. Ingle, on the other hand, was delighted to see another four-legged friend to cuddle up to. The saying 'fools rush in where angels fear to tread' springs to mind as I recall that first meeting of Rudge and Ingle. She clambered straight onto Rudge's head; he wasn't impressed, so gave a warning growl. She did take heed of this message and remained motionless for all of five seconds before continuing on her journey along Rudge's back. Each time she moved, he growled. It took quite some time for Ingle to complete her journey from Rudge's head to his tail, but she didn't give in. When she eventually reached his hind legs and the little bit of space in the front of his bed, there she nuzzled up with him. Why she just didn't creep into Rudge's bed and lie down quietly in front of him in the first place, I shall never know. Perhaps she just liked living dangerously.

Rudge was less than impressed with this continually active dog. As she was only staying with us for a short while, he had to put up with her energetic attentions. I was hopeful that a new puppy-walker would be found soon. After a few days of having Ingle I suggested to my supervisor that she would benefit from having another dog to play with to get rid of some of her surplus energy. A few days turned into a week that turned into two weeks. It seemed that there were no puppy-walkers with dogs of their own available at the time, so I said I would keep her. I began to feel sorry for Rudge as he did not like the liveliness of this pup and had no intention of playing with her. As far as he was concerned, discipline, and a lot of it, was what she needed. Fortunately for Ingle, Errol was still with us and understood the needs of a lively pup, having been one himself. He was happy to do his bit when it came to playing, even though he was fifteen years old by this time.

It didn't take long, just two or three days, for me to realise just how much of a contrast she was to Fenton. She was happy to go outside, and walked confidently and at speed. I could walk her on a lead, but instead of walking in a straight line she zig zagged her way along the pavement, interested in the sights, sounds and smells in the exciting new world around her. At eight weeks old this wasn't too much of an issue, but Ingle didn't change her habit and she was no better at eight months, when she was still distracted by anything and everything we passed.

I have always prided myself on being good at teaching a puppy basic obedience; that is, to sit, to lie down or to stand, then stay in these positions. I had to swallow my pride where Ingle was concerned. I could get her to sit, go down or stand quite quickly, but getting her to stay in one of those positions was virtually impossible. Her bottom stayed on the floor for about two seconds and then she was up again. The words 'wait' or 'stay' meant nothing to her. At six months her basic obedience was no better than most of my other pups at ten weeks.

I nicknamed Ingle 'Miss Impetuous' as, during her stay with us, everything was done quickly and without too much thought. She was also strong on the lead. This combination of strength and impetuousness was particularly dangerous in freezing winter weather. I am not made for icy conditions and can hardly keep on my own two feet in the ice and snow. My pace slows right down as I could easily lose my balance and slip on the icy pavements. My other pups had all altered their pace to match mine when the weather changed, but not Ingle. There were a couple of snowy and icy days that winter when I really couldn't walk her and she had to make do with a run round the frosted garden whilst I held my breath and hoped that any plants growing there would survive the onslaught.

When she was about ten months old, we went on holiday to Cumbria, and Ingle was boarded in the Guide Dogs kennels. I felt that Rudge and I both needed a holiday from her continual activity and impulsive ways. Whilst we were away the decision was made that, instead of coming back to me after our holidays, she would go into the Guide Dogs Centre in Wokingham to start her training.

Throughout the puppy-walking period, my supervisor visits me at home every month. We work together on improving any traits that would make it difficult for the pup to qualify as a guide dog. By the time the puppy goes into kennels the supervisor has a very good understanding of how the dog works and passes this information onto the trainer. I was unsure with Ingle's particular character traits, almost unchanged since she was a puppy, how she would progress through her training. I was not surprised to hear that after a few months she needed a career change. Ingle was just not the dog for the job. She was rehomed and her new owner took her to agility, just the thing for Ingle; with plenty of action and instructions all the way, there was no time for her to get distracted. There was also another dog in the house, this time one who was prepared to play with her, so in the end she found her niche in life.

Puppy Owners' Warning

Puppies   ** see below

~~Tobacco~~ can seriously damage your ~~health~~

** tights, skirts, trousers, shoes, slippers, chairs, tables, carpets, flowers, lawns, doors, vinyl floors, socks, shoelaces, tea towels, hand towels, cupboards, cars, gloves, toys, a good night's sleep, soap, dishcloths, bread, cakes, newspapers, pens, toilet rolls, shaving brushes, patience… in fact anything and everything.

BUT WE STILL COME BACK FOR MORE!!!

By Monica Easton

Irwin; operation and hydrotherapy

"Oh, another 'I' puppy!" I exclaimed. Within a litter all the puppies' names start with the same letter. The person looking after the mother dog, known as the brood bitch holder, will be given the letter for the litter by Guide Dogs, and then makes a list of suitable names for the pups. There are a few exceptions to this rule, one being when a dog has been sponsored; in that case, one pup in the litter will be given the name chosen by the sponsor, regardless of the letter it was allocated. It is much easier to call a dog whose name begins with a consonant as it has much more 'punch' in it than one beginning with a vowel, but here I was with a lovely black Labrador called Irwin, not really my idea of a doggy name, but I got used to it eventually.

It even seemed to suit him. He was much less complicated than either Fenton or Ingle and training progressed in a much more normal way. His basic obedience was good and he took life in his stride. When he was about eight months old I noticed he was dipping a bit on his front right leg. My supervisor agreed with me; so off he went to the vet to have his leg X-rayed. This showed he had osteochondritis, a condition where a small piece of bone or cartilage rubs on the bone in the elbow joint. I think it must feel a bit like walking with a small stone caught in your shoe. He had an operation to remove the offending tissue and then had six months to recover, before leaving me to undergo his training as a guide dog.

I had a set routine to follow to get him back to health. For the first month he had five minutes' lead exercise every day. For the second month, ten minutes a day. For the third month, fifteen minutes a day; and so it increased until his final month with us, and then I could treat him as a normal pup and free run him. I wanted him to have a free run and enjoy it, which he did but I was really worried that he would hurt his leg and undo all the good work that had been done during the previous six months.

Although Irwin had restricted exercise, he still had socialisation training, and I became an expert on five, ten and eventually up to twenty-minute routes to get me to train stations, shopping precincts and anywhere we could sit and watch everything happening around us without walking in the midst of the action. In addition to this restricted walking, Irwin went for hydrotherapy twice a week. He was a little unsure about swimming the first couple of times, but after that he loved it. He had company in the pool with his brother Isaac, who had had the same operation. Irwin was the stronger swimmer and always seemed to make it his own challenge to race his brother across the pool. Occasionally I went in the pool with him. I didn't swim, as the pool was quite shallow, but just walked with him and played ball. Just another experience for a puppy-walker.

Irwin at hydrotherapy

I'm glad to say that all the time, money and effort put into Irwin paid dividends and he qualified as a guide dog. Although he was a good worker he was placed with a gentleman who didn't need to do too much walking, as Irwin's elbow would be his weak point and would be prone to arthritis fairly early in his life.

As it happened, Irwin retired at seven years old due to changes in his owner's circumstances. He was offered back to me as a pet, but as I already had three dogs in the house I had to say "No". He was rehomed with a widower whose wife had been a guide dog owner. He became a companion for this man and together they did fundraising work for Guide Dogs.

Ducks and DEFRA

Our constantly changing menagerie formed an entertaining background to my puppy-walking highs and lows. Having sold the breeding pair of Cayuga ducks and rehomed the remaining two, we eventually replaced them with a pair of Indian ducks. They are black like Cayugas, but are considerably smaller, even a bit smaller than our original Silver Appleyards.

I named the duck Jade because of the lovely iridescent green of her feathers when the light shone on them. Dave, on the other hand, named the drake Baldrick just because he was a great fan of the television programme *Blackadder*. We weren't very observant when we bought the birds because,

Jade and Baldrick

after a couple of days, we noticed that both of them had swellings on the sides of their faces. Jade only had one on one side of her face, just by the beak, whereas Baldrick had a swelling on each side. This made them look a bit like hamsters with food in their cheeks. It didn't seem to affect them at all, although it would have restricted their suitability as show birds. They lived to a good age, Jade being nearly twelve years old when she died. They had shared the free run area and house with the chickens we had at the time and everyone seemed happy with the arrangement.

Baldrick died a couple of years before Jade. I found him dead on the floor of the chicken house one morning. He was about nine years old, a good age for a duck. Normally, I wouldn't have taken much notice, but at the time there was a scare about bird flu. Only a couple of days earlier a swan had been found in Scotland having died of the disease. I phoned my vet to ask for advice and was told to contact the Department for Environment, Food and Rural Affairs (DEFRA). I did this and was told I would be contacted by the person in the area who was dealing with the problem. I phoned David to tell him what had happened to Baldrick, of my subsequent call to DEFRA and that a member of their staff would be contacting me.

After about half an hour I had a phone call from the man from DEFRA. "I understand that you have a duck that has passed away?" I thought it was quite interesting that he used the phrase 'passed away' instead of just 'died'. I quickly gabbled on about what had happened and my fears of having bird flu. Then I heard a little chuckle at the end of the phone and realised the person I was talking to wasn't the man from DEFRA at all, but David having a little joke with me.

A few minutes after David's phone call there was a knock at the door from the real DEFRA man, who had come to look at Baldrick. He reassured me that Baldrick had probably died from natural causes. After all, that is what usually happens to ducks. We went down the garden so that he could have a look at the chickens and Jade. He was fairly confident that

I didn't have bird flu around as all my birds looked healthy but, as a precaution, he took Baldrick with him to Winchester where he would be checked for bird flu. I would be contacted if he showed positive for the disease. I had a fear at the time that the news of Baldrick's death would spread quickly round the village and before I knew it the paparazzi would be surrounding the house and reporting an outbreak of bird flu in Berkshire, so I didn't tell anyone that Baldrick had died until I was certain that I had the all clear and that our birds were all fit and healthy.

Cola, curly girly

Puppy-walking is a challenge, but some pups are more of a challenge than others. Such was the case with Cola. "Would you like a male curly coat retriever crossed with a Labrador and called Clinton?" He was one of four outside-bred pups coming from Ireland. A few hours before he was due to arrive I had another phone call to say that Clinton was actually a bitch called Cola. Knowing that I preferred to walk dogs, my supervisor asked if I was still prepared to have her. As Cola was already in the country and this was an opportunity to walk something different, I was quite happy to say "yes" to this latest challenge.

After a couple of hours Cola was with us. She

was nine weeks old, two to three weeks older than our pups usually are when they arrive, quite long-legged, had a more pointed muzzle than Labradors or golden retrievers and her coat was curly. The latter feature resulted in her being nicknamed 'Curly Girly'.

Cola was an intelligent dog and quick to learn. The trouble was that she learnt both good and bad things very quickly and didn't make any attempt to discern right from wrong. She loved water, and a dip in our fish pond was an essential thing to do the minute she went into the garden. Jumping over the eighteen-inch-high fence that we had put around the pond was no deterrent to her. As far as she was concerned, that was to keep everybody else out of the water. She had a similar attitude to our stair gates, all carefully placed to limit dog access to the main parts of the house. When she was older they were no problem for Cola, and she could jump over them with about a foot clearance. She was definitely a suitable candidate for dog agility if she didn't qualify as a guide dog.

Stealing was another one of her attributes. Anything on a table or work surface was targeted, not just food, so my work surfaces in the kitchen soon became tidier than they had ever been. Tea towels were hidden in drawers and kitchen roll moved to the top of the fridge to ensure its safety. And it all happened so quickly – blink and she would take advantage. She was with me in the lounge one day when she stole and chewed one of the blocks that I was making for a patchwork quilt. All that work gone in an instant. I had only popped out of the room for about thirty seconds, but that was her moment of opportunity and she took it. I repaired the block, but whenever I see it in the completed quilt it always reminds me of Cola. I suppose in some ways that makes that particular block special.

Friends occasionally looked after Cola for me. I warned them of her habits and said, "I just don't want to hear that she hasn't been a thief." I really would have lost my confidence if they had succeeded in preventing her from stealing anything. I gave one friend half a dozen eggs on one occasion when I dropped Cola off, but when I went back to collect her, my friend thanked me for the eggs and said, "What about the bacon?" Apparently, Cola had left the eggs but stolen half a pound of bacon rashers. Another friend listed the stolen and chewed items, one pencil, a picture frame and a credit card, followed by the statement: "I only went out of the room for half a minute." So, it wasn't just me.

When I was walking Cola, I was in contact with the three puppy-walkers of her litter mates, Cocoa, Captain and Cinders. It was reassuring to hear that we were all dealing with the same problems. It didn't help to solve any of them, but it did make me

Cola, the water lover

feel that it wasn't my fault. To give her credit where it is due, she was a lovely, willing dog to walk on a lead, which made up for all her impish ways.

Cola qualified as a guide dog and went to work for a man who lived in Suffolk. He did mention that there were two ponds in the garden and a stream at the end, bliss for a water-loving dog, although he assured me she didn't go in them. What was the secret of his success? I'd like to know. He also mentioned that Cola often wandered down the track at the side of the house if the garden gate was left open. Knowing her agility skills, I had a feeling she was making her escape by jumping the gate.

Her siblings had mixed success. Cocoa qualified as a guide dog to a student, Cinders didn't qualify as a guide dog but was successfully trained as a conscientious sniffer dog, while Captain was rehomed as a pet.

Despite all her waywardness, I was very fond of Cola, as she had character in large measures. If she had needed a career change I would have had her back and taken her to dog agility. I think she would have been a natural at that.

I was very lucky that Cola's owner Stephen kept in touch with me. Every Christmas he sent me a Christmas card and a little update on her. I knew how she was doing, while she was working and in retirement. Recently I received the following letter and, as I started to read it, I knew the ending was going to be sad.

3rd April 2016

Dear Monica,

Cola came to us when we lived in Debenham, Suffolk, and I can recall the day when she jumped out of the trainer's car to greet both me, Peter, Vanda (the retired guide dog) and the workmen who were building the extension to our house. As the trainer said, 'She is her own dog.' We certainly came to realise just how true that was. She was a bundle of mischief who, when let off the lead, would disappear into the woods behind the house and not come back unless bribed to do so. She quickly became top dog over Vanda, and it was quite a tussle when walking with both of them as Cola wanted to charge ahead but Vanda would have none of it and dragged behind, leaving Peter (or me) stuck between the two of them trying to move forward. As time went on, however, things calmed down and they often went off together to explore the woods.

Vanda passed on and we moved to Ellesmere, Shropshire, where she led me around the town and we went for long walks, either along the Ellesmere canal or around one of the many meres surrounding the town.

We moved to Broadstairs just over three years ago and Cola loved to run along the beach and into the sea. She retired shortly after moving here and was joined by Joy. Those two became as thick as thieves. It was usually Cola who took advantage of the kitchen being left for a short while, but both of them enjoyed the spoils of Cola's good fortune.

Cola was diagnosed with lymphangiectasia some while ago, but medication helped tremendously, as did the strict low-fat diet regime, and she enjoyed life to the full – until January of this year when she began to show other symptoms that at first we put down to her scavenging habits. Different medication helped, but over the last months she began to lose weight, became listless and slowed down considerably. She had been on heavy medication for the last three months and, whilst she at first recovered, she regressed, and on Friday 1st April we had to take the decision to put her to sleep. The vet who performed the operation said it was the right decision, and my partner, the vet and his assistant ensured that she slipped off peacefully.

My partner was very upset as he and Cola had shared the same bedroom for over twelve years and had developed

a very strong bond. Our house is quieter now and we miss
her, but we will never forget her. Thank you for looking after
her as a puppy and allowing us to have such a character in
our lives.

   Yours sincerely,
   Stephen

Although I hadn't seen Cola for over twelve years, this letter still brought a lump to my throat and tears to my eyes. It encapsulates all that puppy-walking is about. Although we only have them for a year, our thoughts are with them for life, and to see their personalities continuing into their adult lives and the joy and independence they bring makes the whole job worthwhile.

Dogs and Chickens

"Look!" I said to my brother, "the dog's chasing the chicken."

And she was! Three times round the vegetable patch, chicken followed by puppy, followed by Mum, wings, legs and arms all pumping hard. Then in a flurry of fur and feathers they all disappeared behind the chicken house and the garden was still.

"Do you think it's dead?" I asked. "Well, if the chicken is, the dog will be too," replied my brother. Mum appeared with the dog and then went back behind the chicken house. We waited with baited breath.

"It's OK," said my brother in a relieved voice, "she's put something in the nest box, and she wouldn't do that if it was dead." "It might be injured though," I responded. "If she tells the dog off, it is," was my brother's reply. As if on cue, Mum reprimanded the dog. We looked at each other – "It's injured!"

What followed was a complete obedience session: 'sit, down, stay, come'. "Badly injured," we decided. My brother opened the window. "Is it alive?" he asked.

"What, the dog?" was the curt response. "Just!" (*She was fine really.*)

Well, the chicken survived and so did the dog. All animals have to get on together in our house.

By Julie Easton

Elliot and guide dog training

L ife was much less hectic with our next dog, Elliot. He was black and a Labrador crossed with a golden retriever. Like most Guide Dog bred puppies he came to us after having spent the first six weeks of his life in a home with his siblings and his mother, the brood bitch. Then he was taken to the breeding centre in Warwickshire for a couple of days, where he was checked that he was fit and healthy and was given some early vaccinations before coming to me. He was then ready to start his first year of training in the Easton household.

When he arrived he was a calm and cuddly puppy. He was reluctant to walk on the lead for the first few weeks, so I happily carried him so that he could experience as many different things as possible at an early age. Traffic and busy roads are far less worrying when you are safely cuddled up in your puppy-walker's arms than on the pavement on your own and at the end of a lead. As Elliot grew he developed into a happy, confident and, in general, well-behaved dog, although he was very dog distracted, which could turn out to be his Achilles' heel. He was a big, strong dog, but when lead-walking I could manage him easily; however, if we met another dog I had to react quickly, dig my heels in and hold on tight. Fortunately, this behaviour reduced as he matured.

At fourteen months old the day came for Elliot to leave us and go to one of the main training centres. My supervisor came in the morning to collect him and off they went to the training centre at Redbridge. Once there he was placed in a kennel and run which he shared with two other dogs (he would have liked that) and was introduced to his own personal trainer. It would be another seven months before he would qualify as a guide dog. During the first four months his trainer reinforced the things he'd learnt with me as a puppy-walker, such as basic obedience, walking in a straight line in the centre of the pavement and experiencing as many different situations as possible. What was new was learning to sit at a kerb. In addition, he was introduced to the body piece of the harness he would wear while he was working. Having reached the required standard of work he progressed onto the final three months of his training. He had to take on more responsibility, such as sitting and waiting at kerbs and avoiding obstacles without being asked. Finally, he learnt to cross roads without moving traffic on them, and more importantly not crossing when there was. To make sure Elliot was good enough to be a guide dog, his trainer wore a blindfold and let Elliot guide him as though he were blind. Elliot passed all these tests and was matched with a man who worked in London. This was his first guide dog, so it was a learning curve for both of them.

Early on in his working life Elliot had a problem with the cruciate ligament in one of his hind legs, making walking painful. Following a leg operation, and after a careful rehab period, he was able to return to work. Unfortunately, when he was seven years old he had the same ligament problem in the other hind leg. Another operation and more careful rehab returned him to health, but this time it was decided to retire him. He was rehomed and, among other things, his new owner took him to the local primary school where he sat with her, and his presence encouraged children to read.

Jake retires

It was the letter that we had been expecting.

'Well, that time is approaching; I am going through the re-interview process right now and will be going on the list for a new dog very shortly. Jake is fine, but slowing up a little if I'm honest, and you can never tell. I am concerned that he will simply decide he's played the game long enough one of these days.

This then surfaces; the obvious question of where Jake will live once he retires. The honest truth of it is that I'd do anything to keep him at home but am not convinced that this is the right thing to do. As you know, Jake is a devoted and loyal chap, and I have a feeling he'd be very hurt to see me with a new dog and working a new dog.

So, the big question; admit it, you've been expecting this. Would you be willing to have Jake when he retires? I'd love him to be with people that know him and Rudge – his mate!'

Alastair

Of course Jake could spend his retirement with us. Secretly we'd hoped to give him a home when he needed it.

It was summer 2004 when we went to collect Jake. It is always an emotional time when a guide dog owner has to part with his dog, and this was no exception. In this case, not only was it a working partnership, but these two were 'best mates'.

We didn't stay long. Just enough time to have a quick chat, get Jake's few bits and pieces together, such as collar, lead, some food, a favourite toy and any relevant instructions about feeding, etc., then we were off. Jake happily jumped into the back of our car, which was a mixed blessing. It was good that he wanted to come with us, but sad that he was prepared to leave behind his buddy of eight years. I don't think anyone said goodbye. Jake might have reacted differently if he hadn't known us or if he had been a different breed, such as a German Shepherd, but that is a Labrador for you.

Back at home, it was as if he hadn't been away. He had a few grey hairs around his muzzle and his eyes were a bit cloudy. Cataracts were coming,

Jake, in retirement

which was probably the reason he was finding it difficult to work: all the legs at his eye level were getting hard to negotiate. Apart from that, he was the same well-behaved, fun-loving dog we'd had living with us nine years earlier.

Rudge became Jake's new best mate. The two dogs had got on well together on the few occasions they had met when Jake visited us, and his arrival just cemented that friendship. Daily outings meant fun in the park, walking, running or playing with a ball. Jake went after any ball that was thrown. Rudge was more selective and would only fetch *his* ball, which led to disappointed looks from him as Jake frequently got to Rudge's ball first. Ball throwing became a technical exercise as I had to remember to throw Jake's ball first, then while he was running to fetch it I threw Rudge's ball. That was the only way to guarantee that each dog could came back with his own ball.

As Jake's eyesight deteriorated he began to have trouble seeing his ball. He would follow Rudge instead of the ball, and would end up retrieving the wrong ball. It was at this point that I decided to let them take 'turns'. A maximum of ten goes each to ensure fairness. Jake went first, with Rudge tied to a fence post. Jake kept going until he wasn't able to see where the ball landed, so he didn't always get all his turns. Then I tied Jake to the post and sent Rudge off to get Jake's ball. He had always excelled at playing hide and seek and could be guaranteed to find it. Secretly, I think he had been watching it all the time. It then became Rudge's turn to have his ten throws. After that, game over and home, with two exercised and contented dogs.

"Has someone cut a paw?" Little spots of red on the kitchen floor made me suspicious. A quick check of twelve paws – the pup Elliot had to be checked as well – and everything looked all right, so perhaps I had just trodden on some cotoneaster berries and squished them on the floor. About a week later, there were more red spots on the floor. This time I made a closer inspection of paws and found Jake's outside digit on his back left leg was a bit swollen and oozing some blood. My suspicions were confirmed by the vet. "It looks as if it could be a cancerous tumour," he said. "We can amputate the toe and get the tumour analysed. If the results are positive, and the cancer hasn't spread to his lymph nodes, we can amputate his leg to stop it going to other organs." I crossed my fingers and hoped. Jake had only been with us for a couple of months and this was not the sort of news I wanted to have to share with Alastair just yet. The tumour was cancerous, but the toe was the only part of Jake's body that was amputated. He was happy. He didn't know what the consequences might have been, and I didn't want a three-legged dog.

Life carried on as if nothing had happened. Elliot went to dog-training school in January 2005, Ollie came in June 2005 and sadly Rudge died quite suddenly in January 2006 at nearly ten and a half years old. It started with him staggering a bit when he walked. Initial tests and X-rays didn't show anything in particular. He deteriorated rapidly and after two weeks couldn't walk. I was reluctant to send him off for more detailed tests and decided that the kindest thing was to have him put to sleep. But Jake was still with us, showing no signs of the spread of any cancer. I'm glad I didn't have his leg amputated.

Jake was still enjoying his daily walk, or two if he could get them; the only thing I noticed was that his breathing sounded a bit raspy. It didn't bother him, but I was getting a bit concerned, so off we went to the vet. "It sounds like laryngeal paralysis." The vet named the problem, but I didn't recognise the condition. "He needs tie back surgery to repair it. It is quite a specialised operation and we don't do it here. We can refer him to the London Veterinary College." And so began another interesting journey into the world of veterinary science.

"Yes, we can do that operation," was the response from the college, "but it is expensive." What to do? He wasn't insured and it was a lot of money to spend on a dog, even if he was much loved. I spoke to Guide Dogs' dog care and welfare advisor. She suggested I went to see Tim, the vet who had treated Lynton for his pancreatic problems, as he had some experience of this operation.

What a good idea this turned out to be. Tim could do the operation. He couldn't guarantee that it would be successful, as the procedure involved sewing torn tissue, rather like dealing with fraying fabric. We decided it was worth trying, as Jake was such a lovely dog and otherwise still fit and healthy. It would still be an expensive operation, but I justified the decision in my mind with the thought that as we didn't smoke or drink we could spend the money that other people might have spent on these habits on Jake instead. Travelling to Wokingham also appealed much more than a journey round the M25.

"Bring him in by 8.30 next Tuesday morning. I'll operate that day. He will stay here for two or three days after that to recover," said Tim. Late Tuesday evening the phone call came to say that Jake had had the operation and was recovering well from the anaesthetic. What a relief. The next morning brought another update from Tim. "I'm afraid the flesh has pulled away from the stitches and he needs to have the operation repeated. I will do it for you again today at no extra cost." What a generous offer this was, and this time it worked. The next day another phone call from Tim asking me to go and collect him. I was expecting Jake to be staying at the surgery to recover for two to three days, so I wasn't prepared for that. It turned out that there were two reasons to send him home early: 1) it was August and very hot in the building, 2) probably more unexpectedly, other dogs were barking and Jake was joining in. Barking was not good for a dog that had just had surgery on his throat.

I went to collect him. The boot of my car was open as Tim walked out with Jake. I went to help lift him into the car but, in spite of his time at the vets, Jake was ahead of the game and went to jump in as usual. He did quite well considering he was still a bit dozy from the anaesthetic, but he didn't quite make it and began to fall backwards out of the car. Tim reacted quickly, caught his rear end and rescued him. All of Jake was now in the car. I was amazed. I still don't know how a nearly thirteen-year-old dog could have two operations, which meant two doses of anaesthetic, in two days and be so lively on the third day. Could it just be because he was a Labrador?

That evening we sat in the lounge with Jake, watching the television. Nothing unusual there, you would think, apart from the fact that we had to turn down the volume on the television. It wasn't until Jake returned that we realised how high we had turned up the volume so that we could hear it above Jake's noisy breathing. What a successful operation.

No dogs live forever, and Jake was no exception. He soldiered on quietly for another year, but his hind quarters eventually wore out and we had to have him put to sleep a month after his fourteenth birthday. Another doggy life well lived, and more tears in the Easton household.

Ollie;
something different

While I was puppy-walking Cola I read an article in the Guide Dogs magazine about some new stock that the breeding centre had bought, which included a standard poodle. So an earlier suggestion of walking a poodle wasn't so outrageous after all; I was just ahead of my time. As I read the article, I have to admit to becoming quite excited about the prospect of training a poodle. All breeding stock go through the same puppy-walking process and training as guide dogs. Sadly, this wasn't the time, and Paddy the poodle wasn't for me to walk. The seed had been sown, though. I was keen to hear any news of pups from Paddy's breeding programme, and my supervisor was aware of my interest in poodle puppies.

It was a year later when my luck changed. Elliot had left us, and I was awaiting a phone call from my supervisor to let me know about the next pup she needed to place. The telephone rang and the conversation opened with: "I think I may have made your day. Would you like to walk a labradoodle? His name is Ollie; Paddy is his dad and Hazel is his mum." I couldn't believe my ears. "Are you sure?" She knew how much I wanted to walk a poodle and I just wanted to check that it wasn't a joke. It wasn't. I didn't even have to think about it, my answer was a resounding, "Yes!"

Ollie arrived in July and looked just like a black Labrador pup with a slightly more velvety muzzle. This was a bit of a disappointment as I thought he was going to come all curly, but as he grew he looked less like a Labrador and more like a wire-haired terrier. He had curly hair on his back and wispy, wiry hair on his legs. His tail, which had longer hair than a Labrador's, curled right over his back and almost touched it. His final distinguishing feature was his ginger beard. Julie said that he looked a little bit like the 'Hound of the Baskervilles', but much more friendly.

Ollie; curly tail and ginger beard

I was very proud of my puppy. He was calm, cuddly and very bright. He was quick to learn, and his basic obedience was good from a very early age. Because he was so able, I had to make sure that he learnt the right thing from the start because getting him to unlearn something was very difficult. He did have a problem getting house-trained at first. Instead of relieving himself outside or on the newspaper, he would rush into his bed in the cage to go to the toilet. It took a few days to break him of this habit.

Ollie was one of the best dogs I have walked and was a guide dog in the making. He excelled at everything I taught him, and was responsible and unperturbed by any situation we met. That was until he was about eight months old. It is important to introduce our puppies to as many different situations as possible. Basically, this means that where I go my pup comes with me.

Sunday meant Ollie joined me for a half-mile walk to our local church, an hour lying quietly by my feet during the service and then a bit of socialising with the congregation over a cup of tea or coffee, including an opportunity for people to have a stroke as long as he was being well behaved. Children in particular loved the chance to have a pat and a gentle cuddle with whichever puppy I had at the time.

When he was eight months old I was surprised how Ollie reacted when four-year-old twin girls rushed towards him to say hello. Suddenly my left arm was dragged behind me and Ollie was trying to make his escape from the building. I hadn't seen him or any other puppy react in this way before and it really did take me by surprise. It was something I would need to be aware of.

One morning a few weeks after this experience we were travelling home on the bus from a training walk in Reading. I had chosen to sit at the front, with Ollie tucked neatly underneath the seat and out of the gangway. Opposite us was a young mother sitting on the pull-down seat, with her child in a pushchair facing towards us. The child was very well behaved and just sat quietly in the chair watching Ollie with interest. Ollie found this very disconcerting and it wasn't long before his discomfort started to show. He didn't know how to cope with the situation, so slowly retreated backwards down the gangway to get as far away from the child as he could. I couldn't leave him blocking the gangway and eventually managed to encourage him forward, but he then felt the safest place to be was on my lap. I think the other passengers on the bus must have wondered what was going on. There I was on the front seat with a large dog trembling on my lap. I managed to coax him back down onto the floor, where he sat very close to my legs. He obviously had a problem with small children, and I would need to build some more exposure to them into his training.

During the next six months there were several incidents with children, but only when they rushed towards him to stroke him. He would panic and run to the end of the lead to get away from them. Julie asked me to bring Ollie to school and talk to her class of six-year-olds about puppy-walking. I agreed, on the condition that the children were all sitting quietly on their chairs when I brought Ollie into the room. When I arrived, Julie asked the children to sit down and be quiet. I went to get him from the car, but mistimed my entry and children were still getting to their chairs. He came through the door with me, took one look at all the children, turned round and ran to the door to make his escape. I put him back into the car and brought Jake in to see the children instead. A totally different reaction from him. A big happy smile on his face and a very waggy black tail. In all other aspects of puppy-walking Ollie was a model pupil, but children could be his downfall.

My final week with Ollie as a puppy was a memorable one. I always give my puppies a special goodbye walk before they leave us, so, a week before going to the Redbridge Centre for training, Ollie and I went for a special walk by the River Thames with one of his puppy friends. Both dogs had a lovely time but, like all parties, it ended in tears (for me, really, not him). I was chatting with my friend as we walked along when I noticed that Ollie was rolling around on his back in the grass. This could only mean one thing and so I called him back to me as quickly as I could, using the whistle, although I could already tell that the damage had been done. I could smell Ollie as he hurtled towards me, eyes bright and tail high in the air; my perfect dog had found a large, very smelly dead fish to roll in and he smelt awful. He thought it was a lovely treat. After a quick rinse in the river, which hardly touched the pong, I brought him home and had to bath him, a complete shampoo into the bargain. The inside of the car also needed some attention, and it was quite some time before it recovered from the combined smell of rotten fish and wet dog. Ollie had blotted his copy book and didn't seem to care.

Ollie with his rosette

Two days later we went to the Guide Dogs' Gala Day. I entered Ollie in the 'best-conditioned puppy over six months' competition for the South and South-East Region. My pups had never done well in this event, so I was really pleased when Ollie came first. Perhaps rolling in a dead fish and having a wash in my favourite shampoo might have been a blessing in disguise.

I came back to earth with a bump, as Ollie had to leave me for his guide dog training three days after winning his rosette. He was a very hard dog to part with and I told him that he could come back if he was not suitable as a guide dog, but there was little chance of that as he was so good.

He spent four months at the Redbridge training centre. I was told that his obedience was excellent and his training was going well, but the children issue had shown itself a couple of times and could be a problem if it didn't improve. After that, Ollie went on to advanced training at the Guildford training centre. Again I was told his obedience was great and he was a very bright dog but, after a couple of weeks, the child problem recurred when the trainer walked him past a school at going home time. This had to be solved before doing any more advanced work. I began to wonder if this perfect dog would actually make it as a guide dog.

Secco, another labradoodle

Ollie was one of my favourite dogs and I was really sad to see him go into training. He had been a brilliant dog to walk and had the potential of being a great guide dog, although his phobia of children could be his sticking point, so I couldn't believe my luck when I was offered another labradoodle to walk. This one was called Secco and was a half-brother to Ollie. They both had the same dad, Paddy the standard poodle. Secco was black, like Ollie, but his coat was longer and curlier, more like a poodle. When Secco arrived, Jake had been with us for two years as a retired dog.

Secco, my second labradoodle

The first night in a strange house without litter mates can be quite a trauma for some pups, especially Secco. The first night went something like this:

- 10:45pm – I put Secco to bed in the utility room. He was not a happy puppy and kept barking. I went to bed in the hope that he would eventually go to sleep.
- 11:30pm – I was awake and so was Secco – still barking. I came downstairs and found I had a poo and two tiddles to clean up. I decided to cuddle him until he went to sleep and then put him back in his bed. This had been a successful trick with previous pups.

- 12:00 midnight – Secco started barking again.
- 1:00am – Secco was still barking and getting quite stressed, and I was missing out on my beauty sleep as well. I got up again and cleaned up another poo and a tiddle. He went to sleep on the floor. I picked him up and put him in his bed in the utility room. He started to bark again, but I was firm and told him to be quiet, and he was, for ten seconds. I went to bed again while he barked.
- 2:00am – I gave up, came downstairs, put the sun lounger bed in the kitchen and Secco and Jake lay down on the floor next to me and we all slept until 6am. Then I woke up and took Secco out to go to the toilet.

The second night:

- 10:45pm – I put Secco to bed in the utility room. He barked and I went upstairs to get ready for bed.
- 11:15pm – Secco was still barking, so I decided to move the cage with Secco in it, to make a barrier between the utility room and kitchen, so my pup could see Jake and have company. Jake didn't co-operate with my cunning plan and went to the far side of the kitchen where Secco couldn't see him (I couldn't blame him really). I went to bed to read a chapter of my book in the hope that Secco would have gone to sleep by then.

- 11:45pm – I finished my chapter but Secco was still barking and was a very stressed pup. He was in the cage, trying to get out and into the kitchen. Unfortunately, he had tiddled and pooed in the cage, trodden in it, climbed up the cage with dirty feet and trodden in the bedding. Obviously that wasn't the answer to my problem; the joys of puppy-walking. I left Jake and Secco in the kitchen and took the cage outside to sort it out as best I could.

- 12:15am – I had completed the task. By then Jake and Secco were quiet in the kitchen, so I went to bed to read another chapter of my book before coming down again to put Secco back into the utility room once he was sound asleep.

- 6:30am – I woke up. I was so tired I had fallen asleep reading the book. I couldn't remember moving Secco, so I rushed downstairs in a bit of a panic, fearing that Jake had somehow hurt, or inadvertently smothered, the puppy during the night, but thankfully all was well. Both dogs had had a good night's sleep together and I had caught up on some of my lost shut-eye. Both dogs got up happily to greet me and then went out to relieve themselves as if nothing unusual had happened at all.

- Let it be noted that Chris slept all through these episodes; how about that for support?!

From then on Jake slept in the kitchen and Secco slept quite happily on his own in the utility room. The first two nights of disruption were not repeated. It is very useful having a pet of your own whilst puppy-walking.

Life with Secco was interesting. He was a sensitive dog, as the trauma of the first two nights showed, and this sensitivity continued throughout the time I was walking him. There was no obvious pattern or trigger for it and I never knew when or where there would be a crisis. Ollie's only problem had been his fear of young children rushing up to him, which was something that I could anticipate. Secco, on the other hand, liked to keep me on my toes. He shared Ollie's uncertain attitude to children, but his response was very different. Instead of running away like Ollie did, he barked at them. Barking at children when he was in the street didn't draw much attention to us, unless they were close up and frightened by the noise, but I couldn't say the same when we were in a supermarket. How often do you hear a dog barking in a shop? I would find myself apologising to the parent of the child, while rapidly trying to remove my very loud dog before they were frightened by him. My shopping expedition would come to an abrupt end.

Secco found another reason to bark when two adults with a large multicoloured stripy umbrella and a child in a pushchair got onto the bus we were on. I'm not sure which was the bigger of the problems for Secco, the umbrella or the child in the pushchair. Not only did he bark at the passengers, but the child in the pushchair was not at all happy to meet a dog, especially one that was barking at him, and also reacted in a very vocal way. There was nowhere to take Secco to remove him from the situation, as the bus was heading towards its destination and the child had to stay too. It was probably the most stressful bus journey I have ever experienced and I was glad when we could get off.

The third major crisis came when we were in a bank. A mother and her two little girls were standing by the door of the building. It wasn't the girls who were the problem; this time it was definitely the two umbrellas that they were spinning round. Secco took his usual stance in a crisis and started barking loudly at them. I couldn't calm him down, but I couldn't get out of the building and away from the crisis either, as the umbrellas were blocking the exit. Eventually, I managed to get the mother's attention over the sound of the barking. The umbrellas were put down, the mother moved the girls away from the door and we made good our escape. By then I was feeling very conspicuous. Secco, on the other hand, was relieved that he had made his escape from a very scary situation. Umbrellas were added to the list of 'Scary Things'. I wasn't sure an owner would be able to use a dog that could only work in dry weather.

Interestingly, children were Secco's main problem, just as they had been for his half-brother, Ollie. With my children grown up I took every opportunity to borrow as many of my friends' children as were willing and keen to be part of Secco's training to try and solve the problem. The problems continued, so, when he was seven months old, Secco went to be puppy-walked by a member of Guide Dogs' staff who had three young children. This would give him a lot of exposure to children and hopefully cure him. Secco decided that these children were great to be with and so were some of their friends, but not all of them. This was not ideal for a guide dog who has to be happy with all situations, so he needed a career change, and ended up staying with the family where he was much loved and very happy.

38

Ollie returns

Aweek before Christmas I was busy preparing a meal for Ian and his sighted friend Brian, who were coming to join us that evening, when I had an unexpected phone call from Guide Dogs' rehoming officer Jackie. My brain raced towards which of my previous dogs were nearing retirement and I might be asked to have back or, even better than that, was it Ollie? It was. Jackie went on to explain that during his training he had shown the same fear of children that I had seen. Things had reached a head when a little boy had run up to him in a supermarket and he was cornered. This was a situation he couldn't cope with but was likely to meet again, and the decision was made to give him a career change.

Ollie's fear of children meant that he would not be suitable as an assistance dog for other charities such as Dogs for Good or Hearing Dogs. "So, Monica," Jackie continued, "as Ollie's puppy-walker you have first refusal. Would you like to have him back?" "YES!" was my instant reply. All thoughts of preparing an evening meal now took a low profile. I arranged to collect Ollie two hours later, after the paperwork had been completed.

Chris and I went to collect him at 4pm. I am not a punctual person, but on this occasion there was no way we were going to be late. Ollie was looking very festive, with red tinsel wrapped around his collar. We were really pleased to see him and, more to the point, he was very excited to see us. He did calm down after about ten minutes or so. Ollie had all the attributes in large measure needed to make an excellent guide dog, but in a world with children it was not to be. We were only too happy to have him back and give him a home. I signed the paperwork and acknowledged that I was aware of his problem. As his puppy-walker I knew his phobia well and could avoid putting him in what he considered to be 'a scary situation'.

Once we got back home I did manage to prepare a meal and we all had an enjoyable if chaotic evening. Everyone, including Ian's guide dog Voss, knew Ollie as a puppy and were pleased to see him. Secco was the only one to feel a bit put out by this

Secco and Ollie

new four-legged arrival. 18th December 2006 was a memorable day in my life. What a Christmas present.

I knew Ollie's problem and how to cope with it. If children came to our house, I kept him separate from them by a stair gate. Then he could decide for himself if he wanted to see a child and could keep well away from them if they were scary. I avoided walking him at times when children were going to or from school or playgroup, and would tactfully cross the road if a child was heading straight for us and could be a threat in Ollie's eyes. With these measures in place, Ollie happily settled back into life at the Eastons'. He really was one of the best dogs I have ever trained, with everyone wanting to be the one to walk Ollie.

Spark by name,
but not by nature

After a few weeks' overlap with Secco, Ollie was an only dog for over a year until my next recruit arrived just before Easter 2008. Spark was one of four outside-bred black Labrador puppies, bought by Guide Dogs' breeding centre as potential breeding stock, but I was to puppy-walk him in the same manner as all my other dogs. If he showed potential to make a good guide dog then he would become a stud dog and hence father some of the next generation of guide dogs. If all went to plan it would be quite interesting to be able to puppy-walk one of Spark's puppies in the future.

Having walked many guide dog puppies by this time, I could tell at a fairly early stage that Spark wasn't like most eight-week-old pups. Most of them are lively and play with all their energy until it runs out, then they curl up and sleep, often just where they are, without heading to their bed. They wake up hungry, eat with the same enthusiasm as they play, and the cycle starts all over again. Spark was the very opposite. He was very quiet and reluctant to walk or play, and the lethargy continued as he grew older. It was hard work to encourage him to walk even one hundred yards and he didn't want to go for a free run. He would rather just lie in the garden or in his bed in the kitchen. I also noticed that he was 'dipping' on one of his front legs when he was walking, and that they were not really parallel to one another but in more of an A-formation. The only time he showed any enthusiasm for life was at meal times and in that way at least he was a true Labrador puppy.

House training didn't go to plan. It begins on day one and within a few weeks most pups are clean and dry, although there is always the odd accident. During this time, I always put newspaper down on the floor. The pups go to the toilet on that, away from their play and sleeping areas. As time goes on I gradually make the paper area smaller, greatly reducing the 'Accident Zone'. They soon develop a routine of times when they need the toilet. I use this routine to my advantage and take them outside when I know they will need to go. Then they 'busy' successfully outside, on command, and are given due praise for their efforts. The pup soon indicates when it needs the toilet, I let it out and house training is complete; happy walker, happy dog.

Spark didn't fit into this normal pattern either. He never learnt to go on the paper or learn to ask when he needed to go to the toilet. I'm not even sure he knew when he needed to go. At seven months old he was still having accidents several times a day and was also wetting his bedding, the last thing that any fit and healthy dog, or even young pup, would do.

I felt very sorry for him. I had found it hard enough to persist with training some of my other puppies when their traits were such that it could probably stop them becoming a guide dog, but they had still been able to enjoy life and, with the association's careful rehoming programme, were living happy lives as pets. This time, I was walking a dog that was unidentifiably sick, unhappy and not able to enjoy life at all. Despite several visits to the vet we had been unable to pinpoint his problems or make life any easier for him. If he had been my own dog, I would have had some difficult decisions to make and would have had to seriously consider what I would do with him next. Spark, however, was not my dog. He belonged to Guide Dogs and any decisions were theirs to make.

Eventually, at seven months old, Spark went to the Guide Dogs Training Centre at Redbridge for tests to try and find the cause of his problems. I was hopeful that a reason would be found that could be treated and would enable him to enjoy life. He was at the centre for a few weeks. Tests for diabetes and thyroid problems were negative and he was still very lethargic. His health problems were still not identified and it was decided that a career change was needed. That was the last I heard of Spark. He is the only pup whose eventual home and life I don't know about and is probably the one who caused me the most concern whilst he was with me.

I wondered what had happened to his three siblings, and it was much later that I heard they had also needed career changes for a variety of health reasons. So, Spark had not come from the best litter of puppies and this would make me think twice about buying a pup for myself. I had become very used to the robustness of guide dog puppies. Fortunately, pups like Spark are the exception, rather than the rule, and my next two charges were at the opposite end of the spectrum.

Neal, a pleasure to walk

Spark left me in August, but his successor, Neal, didn't come until the following June. He was another black Labrador bred by Guide Dogs, and came from known, healthy stock. I wasn't sure about his name, but he was such a lovely pup I could forgive him that. It just sounded a bit silly when saying 'Neal, sit' or 'Neal, down'. At least he didn't find it confusing.

He was just the right dog after the traumas of walking Spark. He was another easy pup to walk and took everything in his stride. He had plenty of character, but not too much, and left us with many happy memories. There was one new naughty behaviour I hadn't encountered before. His love of

Neal at six weeks old

chewing. Neal loved his 'raggas'. These are rope-like toys with a knot at each end and are popular with lots of dogs. Unfortunately, Neal decided that the fringes on the two rugs in the hall looked similar and would also be good to chew. They were as good as, if not better than, a ragga. Although generally an obedient dog, 'No!' and 'Leave!' seemed to be words that he didn't understand when he was fringe chewing, so by the time he left us most of the fringes had gone. As the rugs were quite old, I replaced them with two bound-edged rugs. I had learnt my lesson on the delights of fringe chewing. Or had I?

When my next puppy arrived, he started to chew the corners instead. My budget doesn't run to new rugs for every puppy and so I needed to try a new tactic. This time I abandoned verbal commands for the more subtle approach of putting oil of cloves in the most chewable places. This seemed to do the trick and the rugs are still there on the hall floor, none the worse for their exposure to pups and clove oil.

When Neal was twelve months old, Chris needed to have heart bypass surgery. Much as I loved Neal, I felt that I couldn't cope with him and a husband in hospital in London, so Neal left us two months earlier than normal. As he was such a good dog he went to the new London Training Centre to be trained and then become a guide dog who would work confidently in London.

Puppy-walkers are usually invited to watch their dogs working at the end of their training. When I got the invite to watch Neal I jumped at the chance. Neither of us was prepared to drive in London, so we went by train from Twyford station. It turned out to be a simple journey without too much walking, especially as Chris was still recovering from his surgery. At the centre, we met another couple who had also come to see their pup. We compared notes over a cup of coffee and a platter of sandwiches.

When we met Neal's trainer she told us of his progress and then we were taken to watch him work in some of the roads local to the training centre. So that Neal wasn't distracted by us, we were driven by a member of staff in a van, following him and his trainer at a safe distance. He did well and I was proud of my 'puppy'. Back at the centre we were allowed to meet up with Neal, and I'm glad to say he remembered us. We were pleased to see him and give him pats and cuddles. He qualified and was placed with a guide dog owner who lived on the outskirts of London.

This could have been the last we saw of Neal, but it wasn't. We were contacted by his owner, who said how pleased he was with Neal as a guide dog; he sent some photographs of himself and Neal and gave an open invitation to meet up sometime. In return, I sent a selection of photographs of him when he was with us as a puppy. It was about three years before we went to see Neal and his guide dog owner, Jim. He and his wife live in Blackheath, South East London. Interestingly, this is only a few miles west of the area where Chris lived until he moved to Berkshire for work when he was seventeen years old. We went by train, this time from Winnersh station, via London Waterloo to Blackheath, where we were met by Jim, his wife Angie and, of course, Neal. Back at home we had lunch and then went for a walk in Greenwich Park. Chris had been there many times in his youth, and more recently we were there to see the dressage competition at the London Olympics. During the conversation it emerged that Jim had carried one

Jim and Neal in the London Olympic torch relay

of the Olympic torches across Tower Bridge. I was
curious to know why Jim had been chosen to carry
a torch. He revealed that he had been a Paralympic
swimmer in the '70s and '80s and had competed for
Great Britain at three Olympic games, winning five
gold, five silver and three bronze medals. A great
achievement.

We had a lovely day. It was so good to see Neal in a home situation and obviously a much-loved dog, both as a guide dog and as a pet. It really is a perk to see the puppy you walked with their eventual owner in their home surroundings, which I have been lucky enough to experience several times. Many puppy-walkers never hear anything, not even a phone call, from their dog's eventual owner.

Murdoch, my sponsored puppy

Guide Dogs is a charity and is funded by donations. One way to raise funds is for an individual or organisation to donate enough money to sponsor a puppy. In return, they name the puppy and then receive photos and reports on its progress through training. This was the case with my next puppy, Murdoch.

Murdoch was a cuddly pup and easy to walk. He was vocal when young, but by about four months old, when he was starting to lose his first teeth, he had less to say for himself. Every pup seems to have its own area of difficulty in training and for

Murdoch it was steps. Going up and down steps was a bit of a problem at first. Starting with a small flight of steps in a department store, Murdoch needed a lot of encouragement from me and several members of staff, plus a handful of treats, to climb a short flight of five steps. It took about five minutes, but he finally did it amidst plenty of praise from me and the staff. As he grew and practised flights of steps, twenty or more became easy.

When Murdoch was four months old, the BBC television programme *The One Show* was doing an item about guide dogs. Murdoch and two other young puppies were present so the public could view them, through the medium of television, while Dave Stanton, Guide Dogs' breeding stock manager, was being interviewed. A few days later, when I was taking Murdoch into Reading on the bus, the people in the seat behind me mentioned that they had seen some guide dog pups on the television earlier in the week. It made my day, and theirs, to be able to say that Murdoch was one of those three puppies.

Murdoch's training went well and he made his own mark on my life, just as every pup had before him. In my eyes, Murdoch had two distinguishing features: one was that he always put his left front paw in his food bowl when he was eating, to stop it from sliding around on the floor, and the other was that he moulted LOTS of hair, ALL the time.

Murdoch enjoying Henley Royal Regatta

My kitchen floor and all our carpets are a pale fawn, which was lucky as he had such light-coloured hair. I can't think what the floors would have looked like if he had been a black dog, or if my carpets had been darker. As it was, the vacuum cleaner never had a day's rest.

All good things come to an end, and so Murdoch went to the Redbridge Training Centre when he was fourteen months old. When he qualified, he went to work in the Milton Keynes area. I just hope his owner can cope with all the dog hairs!

Ollie, my agility dog

While puppy-walking Secco, Spark, Neal and Murdoch, I had Ollie as my pet dog. He earned his keep as a pet as he helped with puppy training. He didn't accept bad behaviour, and told all my pups what they shouldn't do. He also helped with training friends' pups with recall and discipline. Ollie found it especially difficult to get through to one particular German Shepherd puppy called Kim that a friend was walking. He told her at least four times to leave him alone, but she didn't listen. In the end, he got to his feet and used his size as well as his voice to give a more forceful approach. At last she listened and left him alone. From then on, she didn't bother him, nor did he ever give her eye contact. Instead he would lift his head and look away from her when she came near. Ollie was not impressed with disobedient dogs.

I was also keen for Ollie to do dog agility, which I had done with Rudge. I thought he would enjoy it and would be faster than Rudge, and I was right. No longer could I keep up with my dog as he ran round, so verbal control from a distance was key. Thankfully, Ollie listened well. He knew his left and right commands from his puppy-walking training and that helped a lot. The fact that he could stop inches from a jump when I shouted "No!", if he was about to go over the wrong one, saved us several eliminations. He started with some individual lessons with dog trainer Iain Lewis for a few months until he was good enough to join a class at Cranbourne Agility Club. This was perfect for him and he soon learnt how to approach all the different obstacles.

With all this individual attention, the one thing he hadn't learnt was to 'take turns'. He was used to being the only dog in the class, so now he found it quite hard waiting for other dogs to have their go first. Somebody has to go first, so I usually volunteered Ollie. Then he didn't have to wait for others to have their turn. He was too busy having treats as a reward for his efforts, so he didn't notice while the other dogs were doing the course. I can make treats last a long time. He also thought he should have a titbit when any other dog had run, and would sit begging

Ollie, my agility dog

in front of each handler in the hope of getting a bit of a treat. This was a trick he continued to try out on any handler throughout his agility career, especially if they had better treats than me. He particularly liked cheese and sausages. Ollie won as many clear round rosettes as Rudge, but because of his speed was placed in the top six several times.

His agility career ended when he was just over nine years old. He was having problems with his cruciate ligament and eventually the vet, Lucy, successfully operated on his left hind leg to repair the damage. At this point I decided I would rather have a dog that I could take for a walk than continue with agility and risk undoing all of Lucy's good work.

Copper, a different challenge

After Murdoch left us I decided to have a break from puppy-walking, but that didn't mean I didn't have another pup. For several years I had fancied owning a German Wirehaired Pointer (GWP) so now was the time to get one. They are a member of the Hunt Point and Retrieve (HPR) group of dogs and have very different focus and characters to the breeds I had been used to. I found this out the hard way. I read books about them, spoke to a friend who had them and researched breeders. Perhaps I should have taken more notice of statements such as 'They are challenging, strong-willed and very active dogs.'

Having made a mental note of these points, I ignored them, followed my heart and bought a puppy. I chose a dog and called him Copper. My friend Margaret bought a bitch from the same litter and called her Inca. It was good to know someone with the same breed of dog so that we could compare their behaviour and development.

My next-door neighbour, Catherine, bought a puppy at the same time. She chose a chocolate Labrador bitch and called her Polly. The three dogs went to their first puppy socialising class together. Copper was great with the socialising bit, but concentrating on basic obedience was not his forte. He was constantly dog distracted and hadn't learnt any of the basic commands by the end of the six-week course; and I had felt that teaching basic obedience had been one of my strengths as a puppy-walker. At the end of the course rosettes were presented. Copper got his, more or less, as a consolation prize for my benefit, and he was given the title of Class Clown.

Copper and Polly often played together in Catherine's garden. It is bigger than ours and the dogs could have a good run around and tire each other out – lazy man's dog-walking. It worked for Polly, but Copper still had surplus energy when it was time to come home. On one of these playtimes, Copper had given up playing with Polly, disappeared round the side of the house and come back running round the garden with a furry cat bed. Catherine asked if he had brought it round with him. I said, "No, I thought it was something you had thrown out and put round the side of the house." When I went to see what else he might have taken out of the bin I discovered the side gate was open. Copper had gone out of Catherine's garden, down the road and visited the house next-door but one. He had brought back the cat bed that the owners kept by their front door so their cat could relax in the sun. I was very relieved it was the bed and not the cat.

Copper was a lively pup, a combination of Errol and Cola times ten. Stealing and chewing were high on his list. He destroyed his toys, chewing and eating raggas, rubber dog toys and tennis balls. He stole food off the work surfaces and, as he grew, could even reach food on top of the fridge, which is about five feet high. His stealing was not restricted to food. Anything left within his reach was fair game: pens, coasters, Chris's glasses, cutlery, handkerchiefs, socks, dishcloths and pot brushes. He pulled coats off hooks (the hooks came as well) and chewed through the other dog leads. The list is endless. He not only chewed but also ate several dishcloths and my mobile phone cover. He must have had a good digestive system as they all came out the other end after a couple of days.

Having started basic obedience straight away and discovered that Copper was not a natural, I continued with follow-up classes; at one point we were going to three classes a week, but Copper wasn't listening or looking. It was virtually impossible to get eye contact. This was not good. I joined another local dog-training club when Copper was about seven months old and things started to improve. It was a couple of months later that he passed his Bronze Good Citizen award, quite an achievement, and I was actually proud of him.

The hall where this training took place had a table at one end with a box of dog toys on it and quite often a tub of tasty dog treats such as chicken, liver cake, sausages or dried fish. I tried to keep well away from the table as Copper was very easily distracted by all the food and toys and would suddenly lunge at the table to grab something when we passed. When we had playtime at the end of the lesson we were allowed to take a toy from the table for our dog to play with. I usually chose a fluffy toy for Copper. One evening someone else had taken Copper's favourite fluffy toy, so I chose a couple of other toys, but they didn't appeal to him. In the end, as we were the last to choose a toy, I put the box on the floor so Copper could select one himself from what was left. Having too much choice is never a good thing, and that week he missed all his playing time because he couldn't decide which toy to play with.

At eighteen months old, with a lot of hard work and practice, Copper gained his Silver Good Citizen award. A few weeks later, at the end of term, he was awarded another certificate, which was very apt: 'Class Clown'; we'd been there before!

Copper was in his element on a free run. Our local walking area was ideal for him. There is a recreation ground the size of two football pitches, fields with rough, long grass, small copses, lots of blackberry bushes, a stream, a river and lakes. His first free running was in the recreation ground. He would run at top speed from one side to the other, often with the excuse of chasing seagulls, pigeons or magpies that he saw in the distance. He never succeeded in catching anything because he couldn't fly, but he did get rid of a lot of surplus energy. Occasionally, he strayed beyond the edge of the recreation ground into a small copse backing onto a housing estate. On one of these expeditions after Christmas he returned with a ham bone which he must have stolen from one of the houses. At that point we decided to free run him further away from civilisation in the rough grass area, only entering the recreation ground with him on a lead.

Copper found the long grass, copses and brambles even more fun than the recreation ground. Every walk became an adventure. Because the scrubby area had long grass and tall plants, Copper took to leaping through it. One second he couldn't be seen and the next moment he was in the air, legs stretched front and back with his rather large ears

Copper, flying ears

flowing back behind him. As he matured, his recall improved, and with three blasts on the whistle from me he was heading back at top speed and arriving at my feet in a perfect sit, hoping for a treat. Ollie was never far away from me on a free run, so he would do a perfect recall every time I called Copper. He felt sure he would be given a treat as well, and he was right.

Free runs were never totally relaxing as Copper would usually manage to do something unexpected. One morning when Chris was walking him I had a phone call to say that Copper had found the carcass of a deer and was running around with its hind leg. It was only the leg bone (something else had eaten the meat) and he wouldn't come back. They would be home sometime, but Chris wasn't sure when. Eventually, they arrived without the bone. I don't know how Chris got Copper back, but I suggested that if anything like that happened again he should not get cross with him and, when he eventually came back, praise him for coming, put him on a lead and let him keep his prey. It must have been at least a month before Chris took the dogs that way again, but Copper remembered the deer carcass and this time he chose the ribcage. Following my instructions, Chris kept calm, called and whistled him, and back he came, complete with the ribcage. He walked back with Copper on his lead, proudly carrying his loot, and once he got home he quite happily swopped it for a dog biscuit.

We live near the River Thames and a favourite walk of ours is along the towpath at Sonning. At one section of the towpath there is a steep, wooded bank. Ollie was always happy to walk along the towpath itself and paddle in the shallow parts of the river. Copper found it much more fun to run up the wooded slope, but it was anyone's guess as to where he would come down. It was often at least thirty or forty yards ahead of us, or even behind us. Although we didn't always know where he was, I was beginning to be confident that he knew where we were. It was on one of these walks that I noticed drops of blood on the towpath. "It looks as if someone's dog has cut itself," I said, then realised that Copper, Mr Adventurer, was the dog in question. So a trip to the vet was needed to patch up his cut paw. Copper got himself into so many scrapes that he seemed to be becoming a regular at the vet. This was not his first visit, nor would it be his last. He was always enthusiastic to see all the staff, probably a bit over the top, but everyone seemed equally happy to see him. At least he was a very happy and co-operative patient.

When Copper was a year old, I started dog agility lessons with Iain Lewis, where I had started with Ollie. Being an energetic dog and coming from an intelligent breed, I had great hopes for him. The equipment was at the top end of the field, but Copper's heart and soul were at the bottom end, a long way away, with the wild rabbits. He would do one or two jumps and then he was off to check out the rabbit population. Getting him back took ages, so most of the lesson consisted of Copper tackling three or four pieces of equipment, then running away, with me calling and whistling him and encouraging him back with fluffy toys. Inca was in the same lesson but could concentrate much more on her owner, Margaret, and the job in hand, so she had far more success than I did.

We have friends who live in Surrey near the Devil's Punch Bowl, a lovely area for dog walking. On one visit we parked and let the dogs out of the car. By this time, Copper's recall was very good, so I didn't worry when he went to investigate the wooded slope opposite the car park while we put on our walking shoes. Then we started walking towards a gate next to a cattle grid at the start of our route. We all went through the gate at the side of the grid, including Ollie, thus avoiding the dangerous poles and gaps of the cattle grid. Then I called Copper. He came immediately at top speed. He couldn't see the point of going through the small gate when there was a wide open space to the left, and obviously hadn't noticed the dangerous grid he would need to cross. Still at full speed he reached the cattle grid, too late to stop. He made a last-second decision to leap, and landed safely on the other side. The grid must have been at least ten feet wide, so goodness knows what damage he would have done to himself if he hadn't cleared it. Perhaps agility training had been worthwhile after all. He might not have concentrated during lesson time, but he was quite prepared to apply it to everyday life.

I was determined to persist with agility training my dog, and at two years old Copper joined the beginner's class at Cranbourne Agility Club where I had previously trained with Rudge and Ollie. He hadn't made enough progress to go into a higher standard class like his sister, Inca. This venue offered more challenges for Copper. He was a nosey dog and had to check out all the other dogs in his and the other classes. One or two dogs were a little bit

Copper was developing into a good agility dog

sparky. Copper was not willing to be bossed about, so he would 'swear' back at them, which was not ideal. It was a pity he was so distracted because he could tackle all the obstacles easily, including the weave poles. Just keeping him focused was difficult. A few weeks after joining the club he was awarded a trophy at the AGM for 'The Most Challenging Dog', which was a fair comment. I looked at the list of past winners of the trophy and realised he was in good company. At least it was a step up from 'Class Clown'. I took him to other training lessons for a few months. These were in a fenced paddock and only had one class of dogs running at a time.

He still ran off to start with, but with no rabbits to chase or other classes to distract him he made some improvement. After a few months I could run him around a full-sized course of fifteen to twenty obstacles. At last he was maturing.

Copper had a good appetite and could eat almost anything without it upsetting him. One morning when he was just over two years old, I put his bowl of food down for him, but he just looked at it – very unusual for him. He didn't have his happy-go-lucky face on, and as the day progressed was vomiting and really didn't want to move, so it definitely meant a visit to the vet. Again, being a perfect patient, he stood still and let Lucy examine him. She thought she could feel something hard in his gut and we came home with anti-vomiting medication and instructions to observe him. He wasn't sick, but was still not right. In the night I was woken by Copper groaning. He was in agony. I had never heard a dog make such a noise; he was a sorry sight. The next morning, I was at the vet as soon as the surgery was open. Copper was admitted and X-rayed. This showed a blockage in his small intestine. A decision was made to open him up and find out what was causing his problem. It turned out to be a piece of rubber about the diameter of a fifty pence piece, which was stuck in his small intestine. He stayed at the vet's surgery for three days. When I collected him I was given the offending piece of rubber. I recognised it instantly as the top off a toy rubber dog bone. We had had two of these toys for several years and none of the guide dog pups had shown any interest in them, but Copper loved them and chewed them to pieces. I had thrown out what was left when Copper was about a year old, so the offending piece must have been lurking in his stomach for at least a year before trying to venture further down his gut and causing a major blockage. He recovered well from his operation, but the day he went to be signed off he had a swelling the size of a golf ball on his left hock, probably the result of an insect bite. It took three different types of antibiotics before that was better. I think he just wanted an excuse to be pampered for longer by the staff at the vet's.

At about this time, Catherine decided to let Polly have a litter of puppies. They were due on 7th May and I was asked if I wanted to be around when they arrived, a kind of assistant doggy midwife. I jumped at the idea. I had had twenty-seven puppies from six weeks old but had never been around at the birth of a litter. Catherine phoned me at 8am on the due date saying that she thought Polly was in labour. I quickly had my breakfast, fed my dogs and rushed round next door. By 10.30am nothing had happened, so I felt duty-bound to pop home and give Ollie and Copper a walk before returning to the labour ward. Thankfully nothing happened whilst I was out. It was a few minutes before midday when the first puppy arrived, a big dog weighing over 400 grams. During the day, five more arrived, but none were as big as number one. There were three dogs and three bitches. Sadly, the smallest bitch died after a couple of days, but the remaining five pups were fit and healthy. I followed their progress during the next eight weeks. All had homes to go to and had been given names by their prospective owners. Number one pup, who had a blue collar, was going to be called Charlie Brown.

From when they were about two weeks old, Copper came with me to see and play with them. My worry was that he would tread on them by mistake, but he was very good with the pups. He gently pawed them and other times they ran excitedly around him. In contrast, Ollie came to see them once but decided they were too unruly for him and declined any future visits. All the pups were homed, but Charlie Brown came back after a couple of days. He had an overshot jaw, which needed extensive treatment that his new owners couldn't afford as he wasn't insured at that stage. Catherine decided to keep him and now there were two chocolate Labradors living next door.

As Copper got older, his concentration finally began to get better. At two and a quarter years old, he won a cup for 'Most Improved Dog' at obedience training. By the time he was two and three quarters

Copper was good with Polly's pups

he was making great progress. He loved doing obedience and in the evenings, when I really felt like relaxing, he would come and nudge me to go and do some practice. After fifteen minutes he was quite happy to come back indoors and lie down quietly for the rest of the evening. There was an internal competition at the dog training club at this time and I decided we should enter it, together with about twenty other members and their dogs. Copper was in level three for dogs who had their Silver Good Citizen award. He came first in his group and then won a rosette for Best in Show. He won most points overall and I was really proud of him. He'd come a long way in a year from being 'Class Clown'. At last he was maturing, but it had taken a long time.

Copper, too much of a challenge

Having reached maturity, Copper decided he was going to be top dog. Most evenings I sat on the floor with one dog either side of me, something I had done for years with all my dogs. One evening, quite unexpectedly, while we were sitting like this, Copper suddenly snapped at Ollie. No blood was drawn, but it was very unnerving. Ollie got up and walked away. This was something I would have to keep an eye on. Over the next couple of months there were several incidents where Copper showed his dominance. Ollie was being pushed out, and it reached the stage where he wouldn't come into the room when Copper was there. Ollie hid and kept out of Copper's way. It even got to the stage where I didn't want to put the two dogs together in the back of the car as I could see from Copper's face that he was ready to cause trouble. For my peace of mind, I kept the dogs separate from then on. Ollie was no longer the happy dog that he had been, and Copper had broken the golden rule of the household: everyone has to live in harmony. As with all the other problems that I had had with Copper, I asked for advice from my GWP-owning friend, Alan, on how to solve it. For the first time the answer came back: "This won't get better; it will only get worse."

Reluctantly, I made the decision to rehome Copper. I felt he needed a home where he was the only dog, although he could live happily with a bitch. In fact, having another dog to play with would be great for him, and if there were a couple of acres to run free in that would be ideal. Julie listened politely but was not convinced we'd find a place like that; not many people have a garden that size.

I contacted his breeder and explained my situation, worried about how she would react. Thankfully she fully understood and helped me with the rehoming. She advertised Copper on her Facebook page and vetted all applicants to make sure they were suitable. It wasn't long before a couple from Scotland said they were interested. They lived in a large house, with about two and a half acres of land on the edge of a loch. They already had a nine-year-old, rescued German Wire-haired Pointer bitch and wanted a dog for company. They obviously knew the breed and it all seemed too good to be true. They came to see him on a Friday evening. They liked him, and we and Copper definitely liked them. We agreed that they could collect him on their way home on the Sunday morning. I couldn't part with him on the Friday as I needed time to take him for one of his favourite walks and say my last goodbyes. On Sunday morning he jumped into their car after having a quick check to see if the neighbour's cat was strolling across our lawn. Off he went quite happily, as he always loved a car ride. It didn't bother him that I had a great big lump in my throat and was shedding quite a few tears.

To add to my woes, five days before Copper went, Ollie had an operation for cruciate ligament damage to his left hind leg. The recovery meant restricting Ollie's movements for four weeks. He spent all the time in an indoor kennel or our small utility room, only going out on a lead to go to the toilet. I felt sorry for him, so I sat with him whenever I had a cup of tea or coffee. I am not sure if he appreciated it, but it made me feel better. After four weeks he was allowed to go for two fifteen-minute walks a day. These gradually increased until he was doing two forty-minute walks a day, which was more challenging for me than him. After that, he was declared fit and OK to free run. That was great, but there would be no more agility or chasing a ball, his two favourite activities.

I heard from Copper's owners that he had travelled well on his journey to Scotland and that he was getting on well with their bitch. They were chasing each other around the large garden. He was practising his basic obedience and, knowing that he had done some dog agility, his new owner had made some simple agility equipment and was having a go at that with him. I was happy that he was enjoying life. It was the best thing for him, and me. Life was more restful at home and Ollie was back to his old self, joining us in the evening and sitting next to me again, although it didn't alter the fact that I no longer had an agility dog.

I was on the committee of the dog agility club, but I decided that without a dog to run there seemed little point in me being a member, so at the next meeting I said that I would resign at the AGM. A voice on my right-hand side said, "You can run my dog for me if you like. I have a bad back, so can't work him at the moment. He's a bit sparky with some dogs, so I can hold him between runs." It was a kind offer, but from what I could remember he might have been as challenging as Copper. While I was mulling this over in my mind, a voice from the other side of the table said, "I've got three dogs; you can run one of those if you like. I can only run two in an evening or give two of them half a lesson." I knew these dogs, and they were really good, grade five or higher, but I was only grade one. It was very tempting and I felt quite honoured that the owner trusted me to run one of them, but it didn't stop there. A voice to the left side of me said I could share her dog. A very generous offer, as she only ran the one dog. She was one of Ollie's contemporaries and had often been in the same class as him, and I had run her a couple of times just to try another dog. She was good and quick but, as she was an only dog, it seemed a shame to deprive her owner of the fun of running her.

In the end, I accepted the offer of running one of the group of three dogs I had been offered. A couple of weeks later I was offered the choice of two more dogs to run. Their owner, Iain Lewis, was one of the trainers at the club and he had seven agility dogs. So I ended up having a dog to run most weeks and staying on the committee. I really appreciated the generosity of my fellow dog owners and their willingness to let me run their dogs.

Epilogue

Our pets have given me hours of pleasure. I was quite happy to encourage David's enthusiasm for animals, hence our large collection of assorted pets. I would never have thought about having ferrets as pets, but having had them and reared eight babies I am hooked. I always head to the ferret racing stand at a country fayre so that I can have five minutes 'hands-on'.

After Copper was rehomed, and while Ollie was recovering from his cruciate operation, I was a bit despondent with no dogs to train. Catherine cheered me up by offering to let me train Charlie Brown in basic obedience. Being offered a selection of dogs to run at agility also made my day. It's good to have friends.

Puppy-walking has brought its own rewards. I have several friends whom I met through it. For various reasons, few of us still puppy-walk, but we still have dogs, either a puppy that we walked which needed a career change or one that has retired and whose owner isn't able to keep it. We still meet regularly for a cup of tea or coffee, a dog walk and a reminisce.

And finally, I have friends who are guide dog owners. I am lucky that I have been contacted by all but one person who has had one of my puppies. The phone call is nearly always the same: "You don't know me, but I've got your dog and he's lovely." This may be the only contact I get, but it is guaranteed to bring a tear to my eye and is much appreciated. Some owners keep in touch once or twice a year, or some just send a Christmas card. One has become a lifelong friend. This is what I call job satisfaction.

Acknowledgements

I would like to thank Julie for typing and editing my initial manuscript and Chris for the photographs and his IT skills.

Also Emma Noonan, Janet Pickett and Fred Reece for a mixture of proofreading the original manuscript, many useful suggestions and general encouragement.

Some names have been changed in this book to protect individuals' privacy.